教育部、国家语委重大文化工程
　　"中华思想文化术语传播工程"成果
国家社会科学基金重大项目
　　"中国核心术语国际影响力研究"（21&ZD158）
"十四五"国家重点出版物出版规划项目
获评第二届向全国推荐中华优秀传统文化普及图书

典藏版 · 第一卷

Key Concepts in Chinese Thought and Culture
中华思想文化术语 5

《中华思想文化术语》编委会 编

外语教学与研究出版社
FOREIGN LANGUAGE TEACHING AND RESEARCH PRESS
北京 BEIJING

图书在版编目（CIP）数据

中华思想文化术语：典藏版. 第一卷. 5：汉英对照 /《中华思想文化术语》编委会编. -- 北京：外语教学与研究出版社，2023.12
ISBN 978-7-5213-4878-1

Ⅰ.①中… Ⅱ.①中… Ⅲ.①中华文化-术语-汉、英 Ⅳ.①K203-61

中国国家版本馆 CIP 数据核字 (2023) 第 205212 号

出 版 人　王　芳
项目策划　刘旭璐
责任编辑　赵璞玉
责任校对　王海燕
封面设计　梧桐影
版式设计　孙莉明
出版发行　外语教学与研究出版社
社　　址　北京市西三环北路 19 号（100089）
网　　址　https://www.fltrp.com
印　　刷　三河市北燕印装有限公司
开　　本　710×1000　1/16
印　　张　57
版　　次　2024 年 1 月第 1 版 2024 年 1 月第 1 次印刷
书　　号　ISBN 978-7-5213-4878-1
定　　价　349.00 元（全五册）

如有图书采购需求，图书内容或印刷装订等问题，侵权、盗版书籍等线索，请拨打以下电话或关注官方服务号：
客服电话：400 898 7008
官方服务号：微信搜索并关注公众号"外研社官方服务号"
外研社购书网址：https://fltrp.tmall.com

物料号：348780001

"中华思想文化术语传播工程"专家团队
(按音序)

Scholars Participating in the Project "Key Concepts in Chinese Thought and Culture: Communication Through Translation"

顾问(Advisors)

李学勤(Li Xueqin)　　　　　林戊荪(Lin Wusun)
叶嘉莹(Florence Chia-ying Yeh)　张岂之(Zhang Qizhi)
楼宇烈(Lou Yulie)　　　　　王　宁(Wang Ning)

专家委员会(Committee of Scholars)

主任(Director)

韩　震(Han Zhen)

委员(Members)

晁福林(Chao Fulin)　　　　陈德彰(Chen Dezhang)
陈明明(Chen Mingming)　　冯志伟(Feng Zhiwei)
韩经太(Han Jingtai)　　　　黄友义(Huang Youyi)
金元浦(Jin Yuanpu)　　　　静　炜(Jing Wei)
李建中(Li Jianzhong)　　　李雪涛(Li Xuetao)
李照国(Li Zhaoguo)　　　　聂长顺(Nie Changshun)
潘公凯(Pan Gongkai)　　　王　博(Wang Bo)

王柯平（Wang Keping）　　叶　朗（Ye Lang）
袁济喜（Yuan Jixi）　　袁行霈（Yuan Xingpei）
张　晶（Zhang Jing）　　张立文（Zhang Liwen）
张西平（Zhang Xiping）　　郑述谱（Zheng Shupu）

特邀汉学家（Scholars of China Studies）

艾　恺（Guy Salvatore Alitto）　　安乐哲（Roger T. Ames）
白罗米（Luminița Bălan）　　包华石（Martin Joseph Powers）
陈瑞河（Madaras Réka）　　狄伯杰（B. R. Deepak）
顾　彬（Wolfgang Kubin）　　韩安德（Harry Anders Hansson）
韩　裴（Petko Todorov Hinov）　　柯鸿冈（Paul Crook）
柯马凯（Michael Crook）　　斯巴修（Iljaz Spahiu）
王健、李盈（Jan & Yvonne Walls）　　魏查理（Charles Willemen）

学术委员会（Academic Committee）

白振奎（Bai Zhenkui）　　蔡力坚（Cai Lijian）
曹轩梓（Cao Xuanzi）　　陈海燕（Chen Haiyan）
陈少明（Chen Shaoming）　　程景牧（Cheng Jingmu）
丁　浩（Ding Hao）　　付志斌（Fu Zhibin）
干春松（Gan Chunsong）　　郭晓东（Guo Xiaodong）
韩志华（Han Zhihua）　　何　淼（He Miao）
何世剑（He Shijian）　　胡　海（Hu Hai）
贾德忠（Jia Dezhong）　　姜海龙（Jiang Hailong）
柯修文（Daniel Canaris）　　黎　臻（Li Zhen）

李存山（Li Cunshan） 李恭忠（Li Gongzhong）
李景林（Li Jinglin） 林敏洁（Lin Minjie）
林少阳（Lin Shaoyang） 刘 佳（Liu Jia）
刘 璐（Liu Lu） 刘 青（Liu Qing）
吕玉华（Lü Yuhua） 梅缵月（Mei Zuanyue）
孟庆楠（Meng Qingnan） 裴德思（Thorsten Pattberg）
彭冬林（Peng Donglin） 乔 希（Joshua Mason）
任大援（Ren Dayuan） 邵亦鹏（Shao Yipeng）
沈卫星（Shen Weixing） 施晓菁（Lynette Shi）
陶黎庆（Tao Liqing） 童孝华（Tong Xiaohua）
王丽丽（Wang Lili） 王 琳（Wang Lin）
王明杰（Wang Mingjie） 王维东（Wang Weidong）
王 鑫（Wang Xin） 温海明（Wen Haiming）
吴根友（Wu Genyou） 吴礼敬（Wu Lijing）
夏 晶（Xia Jing） 谢远笋（Xie Yuansun）
辛红娟（Xin Hongjuan） 徐明强（Xu Mingqiang）
徐亚男（Xu Yanan） 许家星（Xu Jiaxing）
严学军（Yan Xuejun） 张 静（Zhang Jing）
张子尧（Zhang Ziyao） 章思英（Zhang Siying）
章伟文（Zhang Weiwen） 赵 桐（Zhao Tong）
赵 悠（Zhao You） 郑 开（Zheng Kai）
周云帆（Zhou Yunfan） 朱绩崧（Zhu Jisong）
朱良志（Zhu Liangzhi） 朱 渊（Zhu Yuan）
左 励（Zuo Li）

前言

"中华思想文化术语"的定义可以表述为：由中华民族所创造或构建，凝聚、浓缩了中华哲学思想、人文精神、思维方式、价值观念，以词或短语形式固化的概念和文化核心词。它们是中华民族几千年来对自然与社会进行探索和理性思索的成果，积淀着中华民族的历史智慧，反映中华民族最深沉的精神追求以及理性思索的深度与广度；其所蕴含的人文思想、思维方式、价值观念已经作为一种"生命基因"深深融于中华子孙的血液，内化为中华民族共同的性格和信仰，并由此支撑起中华数千年的学术传统、思想文化和精神世界。它是当代中国人理解中国古代哲学思想、人文精神、思维方式、价值观念之变化乃至文学艺术、历史等各领域发展的核心关键，也是世界其他国家和民族了解当代中国、中华民族和海外华人之精神世界的钥匙。

当今世界已进入文化多元与话语多极时代。世界不同区域、不同国家、不同民族的文明，其流动融合之快、之广、之深超过历史任何时期。每个国家和民族都有自己独具的思想文化和话语体系，都应在世界文明、世界话语体系中占有一席之地，得到它应有的地位和尊重。而思想文化术语无疑是一个国家和民族话语体系中最核心、最本质的部分，是它的思想之"髓"、文化之"根"、精神之"魂"、学术之"核"。越来越多的有识之士认识到，中华思想文化蕴藏着解决当今人类所面临的许多难题的重要启示，中华民族所倡导的"厚德载物""道法自然""天人合一""和而不同""民惟邦本""经世致用"等思想，以及它所追求的"协和万邦""天下一家"、世界"大同"，代表了当今世界文明的发展趋势，也因此成为国际社会的共识。越来越多的外国学者和友人对中华思想文化及其术语产生浓厚的兴趣，希望有更全面、更进一步的了解。

今天我们整理、诠释、翻译、传播中华思想文化术语，目的是立足于中华思想文化，通过全面系统的整理与诠释，深度挖掘其中既能反映中华哲学思想、人文精神、思维方式、价值观念、文化特征，又具跨越时空、超越国度之意义，以及富有永恒魅力与当代价值的含义和内容，并将其译成英语等语言，让世界更客观、更全面地认识中国，了解中华民族的过去和现在，了解当代中国人及海外华人的精神世界，从而推动国家间的平等对话及不同文明间的交流借鉴。

中华思想文化术语的整理、诠释和英语翻译得到了中国教育部、中国国际出版集团、中央编译局、北京大学、中国人民大学、武汉大学、北京外国语大学等单位的大力支持，得到了叶嘉莹、李学勤、张岂之、林戊荪、楼宇烈、王宁等海内外众多知名学者的支持。需要说明的是，"中华思想文化术语"这个概念是首次提出，其内涵和外延还有待学界更深入的研究；而且，如此大规模地整理、诠释、翻译中华思想文化术语，在中国也是首次，无成例可循。因此，我们的诠释与翻译一定还有待完善的地方，我们会及时吸纳广大读者的意见，不断提高术语诠释与翻译的质量。

2021年12月11日

Foreword

By "key concepts in Chinese thought and culture" we mean concepts and keywords or phrases the Chinese people have created or come to use and that are fundamentally pertinent to Chinese philosophy, humanistic spirit, way of thinking, and values. They represent the Chinese people's exploration of and rational thinking about nature and society over thousands of years. These concepts and expressions reflect the Chinese people's wisdom, their profound spiritual pursuit, as well as the depth and width of their thinking. Their way of thinking, values, and philosophy embodied in these concepts have become a kind of "life gene" in Chinese culture, and have long crystallized into the common personality and beliefs of the Chinese nation. For the Chinese people today, they serve as a key to a better understanding of the evolutions of their ancient philosophy, humanistic spirit, way of thinking, and values as well as the development of Chinese literature, art, and history. For people in other countries, these concepts open the door to understanding the spiritual world of contemporary China and the Chinese people, including those living overseas.

In the era of cultural diversity and multipolar discourse today, cultures of different countries and civilizations of different peoples are integrating faster, in greater depth, and on a greater scope than ever before. All countries and peoples have their own systems of thought, culture, and discourse, which should all have their place in the civilization and discourse systems of the world. They all deserve due respect. The concepts in thought and culture of a country and its people are naturally the most essential part of their discourse. They constitute the marrow of a nation's thought, the root of its culture, the soul of its spirit, and the core of its scholarship. More and more people of vision have come to recognize the inspirations Chinese thought and culture might offer to help resolve many difficult problems faced by mankind. The Chinese hold that a man should "have ample virtue and carry all things," "Dao operates naturally," "heaven and man are united as one," a man of virtue seeks "harmony but not uniformity," "people are the foundation of the state," and "study of ancient classics should meet present needs." The Chinese ideals such as "coexistence of all in harmony," "all the people under heaven are one family," and a world of "universal harmony" are drawing increasing attention among the international community. More and more international scholars and friends have become interested in learning and better understanding Chinese thought and culture in general, and the relevant concepts in particular.

In selecting, explaining, translating, and sharing concepts in Chinese thought and culture, we have adopted a comprehensive and systematic approach. Most of them not only reflect the characteristics of Chinese philosophy, humanistic spirit, way of thinking, values, and culture, but also have significance and/or implications that transcend time and national boundaries, and that still fascinate present-day readers and offer them food for thought. It is hoped that the translation of these concepts into English and other languages will help people in other countries to gain a more objective and more rounded understanding of China, of its people, of its past and present, and of the spiritual world of contemporary Chinese. Such understanding should be conducive to promoting equal dialogue between China and other countries and exchanges between different civilizations.

The selection, explanation, and translation of these concepts have been made possible thanks to the support of the Ministry of Education, China International Publishing Group, the Central Compilation and Translation Bureau, Peking University, Renmin University of China, Wuhan University, and Beijing Foreign Studies University, as well as the support of renowned scholars in China and abroad, including Florence Chia-ying Yeh, Li Xueqin, Zhang Qizhi, Lin Wusun, Lou Yulie, and Wang Ning.

The idea of compiling key concepts in Chinese thought and culture represents an innovation and the project calls much research and effort both in connotation and denotation. Furthermore, an endeavor like this has not been previously attempted on such a large scale. Lack of precedents means there must remain much room for improvement. Therefore, we welcome comments from all readers in the hope of better fulfilling this task.

December 11, 2021

目录
Contents

1. àirén-wéidà 爱人为大
   Caring for Others Is the Top Priority 1

2. ānpín-lèdào 安贫乐道
   Be Content with a Simple but Virtuous Life 2

3. bāyīn-kèxié 八音克谐
   Harmonious Combination of Eight Sounds 4

4. běiqǔ 北曲
   Northern Opera 5

5. bīngqiángzémiè 兵强则灭
   Relying on Force and Flaunting One's Superiority Leads to
   Destruction 8

6. bóshī-jìzhòng 博施济众
   Deliver Extensive Benefits to the People and Relieve the Suffering
   of the Poor 10

7. bùyánzhījiào 不言之教
   Influence Others Without Preaching 11

8. cángfùyúmín 藏富于民
   Keep Wealth with the People 12

9. chéngzhúyúxiōng 成竹于胸
   Have a Complete Image of the Bamboo Before Drawing It / Have a
   Fully Formed Picture in the Mind's Eye 14

10. chuánshén-xiězhào 传神写照
    Convey the Spirit and Capture the Person 16

11 chūnjié 春节
Spring Festival 17

12 dàxué 大学
Daxue (Great Learning) 19

13 duótāi-huàngǔ 夺胎换骨
Express the Ideas in Earlier Literary Works in a New Way 21

14 fǎ yǔ shí biàn, lǐ yǔ sú huà 法与时变，礼与俗化
Laws Change Along with Evolving Times; Rites Shift Along
with Changing Customs. 23

15 fǎnqiúzhūjǐ 反求诸己
Introspection 25

16 fēngròu-wēigǔ 丰肉微骨
Fleshy Body and Soft Bone Structure 27

17 gǎnwù 感物
Sensed Externalities 29

18 guāng'érbùyào 光而不耀
Bright but Not Dazzling 30

19 hé tóngyì 合同异
Unify Similarity and Difference 31

20 hé chūyú shì 和出于适
Harmony Comes from Appropriateness. 32

21 hòujī-bófā 厚积薄发
   Build Up Fully and Release Sparingly 33

22 huàxìng-qǐwěi 化性起伪
   Transform Intrinsic Evil Nature to Develop Acquired Nature of
   Goodness 34

23 huàn zhōng yǒu zhēn 幻中有真
   Truth in Imagination 36

24 huìhuà liù fǎ 绘画六法
   Six Rules of Painting 38

25 huì shì hòu sù 绘事后素
   The White Silk First, the Painting Afterwards / Beauty from
   Natural Simplicity 40

26 jīshàn-chéngdé 积善成德
   Moral Character Can Be Built by Accumulating Goodness................42

27 jísī-guǎngyì 集思广益
   Pool Wisdom of the People 43

28 jiǎngxìn-xiūmù 讲信修睦
   Keep Good Faith and Pursue Harmony 44

29 jiéqì 节气
   The Twenty-four Solar Terms 45

30 jìnzhōng-bàoguó 尽忠报国
   Be as Loyal as One Can Be and Serve One's Own Country 47

31 jīng / quán 经 / 权
Constant and Temporary 49

32 jūnzǐ-gùqióng 君子固穷
A Man of Virtue Maintains His Ideals Even in Frustrations................ 50

33 kēzhèng měng yú hǔ 苛政猛于虎
Tyranny Is Fiercer than a Tiger. 51

34 kǔyín 苦吟
Painstaking Versification 53

35 kuāshì 夸饰
Exaggeration and Embellishment 54

36 lètiān-zhīmìng 乐天知命
Rejoice in Complying with Heaven and Know Its Mandate................ 55

37 lí jiānbái 离坚白
Separate Hardness from Whiteness 56

38 líxíng-désì 离形得似
Transcend the Outer Form to Capture the Essence 57

39 lìcí 丽辞
Ornate Parallel Style 59

40 línyuān-lǚbó 临渊履薄
Be Discreet as if Standing on Cliff Edge or Treading on Thin Ice 60

41 liùguān 六观
Six Criteria 61

42 liùyì 六艺
The Six Arts 63

43 máodùn 矛盾
Paradox of the Spear and the Shield / Contradiction 64

44 mǐ bù yǒu chū, xiǎn kè yǒu zhōng 靡不有初，鲜克有终
All Things Have a Beginning, but Few Can Reach the End. 66

45 miàosuàn 庙算
Court Calculation 67

46 míngdé 明德
Illustrious Virtue 68

47 míngfèn-shǐqún 明分使群
Proper Ranking Leads to Collaboration. 69

48 mùjī-dàocún 目击道存
See the Way with One's Own Eyes 71

49 nánxì 南戏
Southern Opera 73

50 nǐróng-qǔxīn 拟容取心
Compare Appearances to Grasp the Essence 75

51 nián 年
Lunar Year / Year 77

52 pǐntí 品题
Make Appraisals 78

53 qízhèng 奇正
Qi or Zheng (Surprise or Normal) 80

54 qìyùn 气韵
Artistic Appeal 83

55 qiānlǐzhīxíng, shǐyúzúxià 千里之行，始于足下
A Journey of a Thousand Li Begins with the First Step. 85

56 qiānxiǎng-miàodé 迁想妙得
Inspirational Creation Based on Association in Thinking 86

57 qīnqīn 亲亲
Affection for One's Kin 88

58 qīngmíng 清明
The Qingming Festival 89

59 qióng zé biàn, biàn zé tōng, tōng zé jiǔ
穷则变，变则通，通则久
Extreme – Change – Continuity 91

60 qiútóng-cúnyì 求同存异
Seek Common Ground While Setting Aside Differences 92

61 sānxǐng-wúshēn 三省吾身
Reflect on Oneself Several Times a Day 93

62 shàngbīng-fámóu 上兵伐谋
The Best Strategy in Warfare is to Foil the Enemy's Strategy. 95

63 shěshēng-qǔyì 舍生取义
Give One's Life to Uphold Righteousness 96

64 shěnyīn-zhīzhèng 审音知政
Assess Governance by Listening to Music 97

65 shēngxiào 生肖
The Chinese Zodiac / Animal of the Year 99

66 shínián-shùmù, bǎinián-shùrén 十年树木，百年树人
It Takes Ten Years to Grow Trees and a Hundred Years to Nurture Talents. 100

67 shí 时
Time / Timing 101

68 shíxù 时序
Change Along with Times 102

69 shǐ 史
History 104

70 shìwài-táoyuán 世外桃源
Land of Peach Blossoms / Land of Idyllic Beauty 106

71 suìhán-sānyǒu 岁寒三友
Three Friends of Winter / Steadfast, Loyal Friends 107

72 tāshānzhīshí, kěyǐ-gōngyù 他山之石，可以攻玉
Use Stones from Another Mountain to Polish One's Jade 109

17

73 tiānlài 天籁
   Sounds of Nature 110

74 tuī'ēn 推恩
   Extend Benevolence and Love 111

75 tuījǐ-jírén 推己及人
   Put Oneself in Another's Place 112

76 xǐmù-lìxìn 徙木立信
   Establish One's Credibility by Rewarding People for Moving a Log ... 114

77 xiànsù-bàopǔ 见素抱朴
   Maintain Originality and Embrace Simplicity 116

78 xiāosǎn-jiǎnyuǎn 萧散简远
   Natural, Leisurely, Simple yet Profound 117

79 xīntóng-lǐtóng 心同理同
   People of Similar Natures and Emotions Will Have Similar
   Understanding. 119

80 xīnyuè-chéngfú 心悦诚服
   Be Completely Convinced and Follow Willingly 121

81 xìn 信
   Good Faith 122

82 xíngjù-shénshēng 形具神生
   Physical Form Gives Birth to Spirit. 123

83 xìngfèn 性分
   Natural Attribute 124

84 xiūyǎng-shēngxī 休养生息
   Recover from a Social Upheaval and Restore Production / Develop Economy and Increase Population 125

85 xiūcí-lìchéng 修辞立诚
   Establish Credibility Through Careful Choice of Words 127

86 xiūdé-zhènbīng 修德振兵
   Cultivate Virtue and Strengthen the Army 129

87 xuándé 玄德
   Inconspicuous Virtue 130

88 xuánliáng-cìgǔ 悬梁刺股
   Tie One's Hair on the House Beam and Jab One's Side with an Awl to Keep Oneself from Falling Asleep while Studying 131

89 yán bì xìn, xíng bì guǒ 言必信，行必果
   Promises Must Be Kept; Actions Must Be Resolute. 133

90 yīyán-xīngbāng 一言兴邦
   A Single Remark Makes a Country Prosper. 135

91 yīyǐguànzhī 一以贯之
   Observe a Fundamental Principle Throughout One's Pursuit 136

92 yǐnshuǐ-sīyuán 饮水思源
   When Drinking Water, One Must Not Forget Its Source. 138

19

93 yǒng 勇
Courage 139

94 yúgōng-yíshān 愚公移山
The Foolish Old Man Who Moved the Mountains 140

95 yǔshí-xiéxíng 与时偕行
Go with the Times 142

96 yuèjiào 乐教
Music Education 144

97 záobì-jièguāng 凿壁借光
Borrow Light from a Next Door Neighbor 145

98 zhèngshēng 郑声
The Music of the State of Zheng 146

99 zhīcháng-dábiàn 知常达变
Master Both Permanence and Change 148

100 zhì 智
Intelligence 149

术语表 List of Concepts 151

中国历史年代简表 A Brief Chronology of Chinese History 157

20

àirén-wéidà 爱人为大

Caring for Others Is the Top Priority.

友爱他人、爱护他人最为重要。古人认为，天地之间，人最宝贵，所以"仁者爱人"。将"爱人"由道德情感层面推及到国家层面就体现为"爱民"。人民是国家的根本，决定着国家的安危与成败，所以统治者要把爱民、亲民、利民、顺应民心作为治国理政的最高原则。制定政策、法律，确立制度，都以保障人民的利益为出发点和最终目的。它不仅是儒家"仁政"思想的体现，也是法家制定法律、依法治国的重要理念，它彰显了中华民族崇高的人文情怀。

Being friendly and caring for others is most important. Ancient Chinese believed that human beings are most precious things in the world, so benevolent people care for others. When it comes to governing a country, a ruler's love for others should be transformed into love for the people. People are the most fundamental components of a state whose stability and security depend on its people. Therefore, a ruler should consider it his top priority to have love for his people, to be considerate to his people, to always make things easier for his people and follow his people's will. Policies should be made in the interest of the people, and so should laws and institutions. This is not only what a benevolent government that Confucianism advocates is all about, it is also the basic concept on which ancient legalists made policies and laws for running a country. It epitomizes Chinese people's humanitarian sentiments.

引例 Citations：

◎欲人之爱己也，必先爱人；欲人之从己也，必先从人。(《国语·晋语四》)

（想要他人对自己友爱，一定先对他人友爱；想要他人遵从自己，一定先要遵从他人。）

If you want others to care about you, you must first care about others; if you want others to comply with you, you must first comply with others. (*Discourses on Governance of the States*)

◎ 君子所以异于人者，以其存心也。君子以仁存心，以礼存心。仁者爱人，有礼者敬人。爱人者人恒爱之，敬人者人恒敬之。(《孟子·离娄下》)

（君子之所以不同于一般人，在于心中存有的想法不同。君子心中总是想着仁，想着礼。仁者爱别人，有礼节的人尊敬别人。爱别人的人，别人总也爱他；尊敬别人的人，别人总也尊敬他。）

Men of virtue are different from ordinary people because they think differently. They have benevolence and propriety on their mind. Benevolent people care for others, and courteous people show respect for others. Those who care about others can always be cared about by others; those who show respect for others will always be respected by others. (*Mencius*)

◎ 古之为政，爱人为大。(《礼记·哀公问》)

（古代的为政之道，以爱民最为重要。）

Caring for the people was the most important part of running a country in ancient times. (*The Book of Rites*)

ānpín-lèdào 安贫乐道

Be Content with a Simple but Virtuous Life

安于贫困而乐于守道。在孔子（前551—前479）与儒家看来，对于道义的学习与执守，并不是出于任何功利的目的，而是发自内心的认同，是毕生追求的最高目标。因此，以道义为最高准则的人，不会以违背道义的方式去追求富贵，即便在物质生活上陷于贫困，也能够以执守道义为乐。

When leading a poor life, one should still stick to moral principles. Confucius (551-479 BC) and Confucian scholars believe that it is not for fame and wealth that one should observe moral principles. Rather, such observance comes from one's heart and represents his lifetime pursuit. So those who are guided by high moral standards will never seek wealth and fame at the expense of justice, and they can live up to such standards even when they live in poverty.

引例 Citations：

◎子曰："贤哉，回也！一箪食，一瓢饮，在陋巷，人不堪其忧，回也不改其乐。贤哉，回也！"（《论语·雍也》）

（孔子说："颜回真是有贤德啊！一筐饭食，一瓢饮水，居住在简陋的巷子里，别人都忍受不了这种忧苦，颜回却不改变自有的快乐。颜回真是有贤德啊！"）

Confucius said: "Virtuous indeed is Yan Hui! He has simple meals, just drinks cold water, and lives in a humble alley. While others would find such living unbearable, Yan Hui remains cheerful. What a virtuous man!" (*The Analects*)

◎子贡曰："贫而无谄，富而无骄，何如？"子曰："可也。未若贫而乐，富而好礼者也。"（《论语·学而》）

（子贡说："贫穷而不谄媚，富有而不骄纵，怎么样？"孔子说："可以了。但不如贫穷而乐于道，富有而喜好礼。"）

Zigong said: "One does not fawn on others when being poor; one is not arrogant when being rich. How do you find such quality?" Confucius said: "Good!

But it is even better to be poor and upright and to be rich and courteous." (*The Analects*)

bāyīn-kèxié 八音克谐

Harmonious Combination of Eight Sounds

八类乐器所演奏的声音能够协调配合，在整体上达到和谐。"八音"指由金、石、土、革、丝、木、匏、竹等八种材质制成的乐器所演奏出的不同声音。"八音克谐"的说法出自《尚书》。它强调发挥八音各自的长处，在整体协调、多样统一中臻于化境，体现了中国古典音乐及词曲创作中以"和"为美的审美追求。而音乐又与人的心灵相通，"八音"能够呈现或感动不同的心灵状态，故而它也成为古代教化的一种方式。其意在于使人心在不同乐声的影响下达到同样和谐的状态，以符合礼乐对于人的心灵与行为的要求；同时它也蕴含不同的人或群体都能发声，但须遵守共同规范、相互配合而能和谐共处之意。

Different sounds produced when eight musical instruments made of gold, stone, earth, leather, silk, wood, gourd and bamboo are played together create harmonious music. This term comes from *The Book of History*. The term, which stresses that different tunes produced by the eight musical instruments should be blended in a harmonious way to create beautiful melody, epitomizes the pursuit of harmony of ancient Chinese music. Music gives expression to people's sentiments; the eight different sounds relate to people's different frames of mind, and can become a way of enlightenment. The term means that people can achieve peace of mind by listening to different kinds of music and should think and act in keeping with what the rites and music require of them. The phrase also implies that different people and groups can all voice their views, but should abide by common rules so as to maintain harmonious ties among them.

引例 Citation：

◎ 诗言志，歌永言，声依永，律和声。八音克谐，无相夺伦，神人以和。（《尚书·舜典》）

（诗是表达内心志向的，歌是用语言吟唱的，五音（宫、商、角、徵、羽）的高低变化要随吟唱而定，音律则要与五音谐和。八类乐器所演奏的音乐能够和谐配合，不要相互扰乱彼此的秩序，那么神与人都能依此进入和谐的状态。）

Poems express aspirations deep in one's heart, whereas songs are verses for chanting. Undulation of tunes of five notes depends on chanting, and meter and melody must be in harmony with the five notes. If the sounds from the eight different music instruments create harmonious music without interfering with each other, such music enables both gods and man to enter a state of harmony. (*The Book of History*)

běiqǔ 北曲

Northern Opera

起源于北方的戏剧。北曲的源头是北宋甚至更早时期流行于北方民间的曲子，配合曲子的词多滑稽浅俗。南宋以后，北方地区在金、元统治之下，女真、蒙古等族的歌舞与音乐元素被大量引入，逐渐形成了独特的北曲体系，同时逐渐吸引了文人加入创作队伍，从而产生了大量优秀作品。与宋代文人词相比，北曲朴素率真，多用口语，格律调式更加自由。其主要演唱形式为小令和套数。用北曲演唱的戏曲形式为杂剧。元代文人社会地位低下，借助北曲抒情寄意，创作盛况空前，代表人物有关汉卿、马致远（1251?—1321后）、白朴（1226—1306后）、郑光祖（?—1324前），被称为"元曲四大家"。

Beiqu (北曲), the Northern Opera, originated in northern China. It was based on northern folk songs that were popular in the Northern Song Dynasty or earlier, and its lyrics were often funny and simple. After the Southern Song Dynasty, northern China fell under the rule of the Jin and Yuan dynasties. As a result, songs, dances, and musical elements of Nüzhen, Mongolian and other ethnic groups were widely incorporated into the Northern Opera, making it a unique form of opera. At the same time, many writers became interested in the Northern Opera and wrote large numbers of excellent opera works. Compared with the lyrics of the literati of the Song period, the Northern Opera was simple, direct and sincere, and there was greater freedom in arranging rhythm. The Northern Opera was performed mainly in the form of short lyrics and cycles. As they dealt with various social themes, operas performed in this artistic form were referred to as zaju (杂剧 opera of various themes). Writers in the Yuan Dynasty had low social status, so they wrote a large number of Northern Opera works to express their emotions and views. They are represented by Guan Hanqing, Ma Zhiyuan (1251?-1321?), Bai Pu (1226-1306?) and Zheng Guangzu (?-1324?), collectively known as the top four Yuan Opera writers.

引例 Citations：

◎宋世所谓诗余，金元以来所传南北曲者，虽非古之遗音，而犹有此名目也，夫人能为之，而闻之者亦能辨别其是否，诚因今而求之古，循俗而入于雅……因声以考律，正律以定器，三代之乐亦可复矣。（丘濬《大学衍义补》卷四十四）

（宋代所说的词，金元以来所流行的南曲、北曲，虽然不是上古留传下来的音乐，但仍然有宫、商、角、徵、羽这些名目，有人能够制作这些曲子，而听曲子的人也能听得出音律是否正确，其实这是从当代音乐推求古代音乐，由俗乐而进入雅乐……凭所唱的声音来考求音律，再通过标准的音律来确定乐器的声音，如此则夏、商、周三代的音乐都可以复原了。）

Song Dynasty *ci* poetry and the Southern and Northern operas that were popular from the Jin and Yuan dynasties onwards were not music from ancient times, but they were still divided into Do, Re, Mi, Sol and La. Some people could produce these kinds of music, and the audience could also tell if it had the right rhyme. Actually, what was done was to restore ancient music based on current music and make popular music more refined… Rhymes were evaluated through singing, the sound of musical instruments was then determined according to standard rhymes, and this made it possible to restore the music of the Xia, Shang, and Zhou dynasties. (Qiu Jun: *Supplement to the Exposition on The Great Learning*)

◎唱者只二人，末泥主男唱，旦儿主女唱。他若杂色入场，第有白无唱，谓之"宾白"。"宾"与"主"对，以说白在"宾"，而唱者自有"主"也。至元末明初，改北曲为南曲，则杂色人皆唱，不分宾主矣。（毛奇龄《西河词话》卷二）

（演唱的只有两个人，末泥专唱男角，旦儿专唱女角。其他角色入场，只有说白而没有唱腔，称为"宾白"。"宾"和"主"相对，说白属于"宾"的事情，演唱则属于"主"的事情。到了元末明初，北曲受南曲影响而改变，则所有的角色都演唱，不再区分"宾"和"主"了。）

Only two people sang in the performance. One was the male character and the other was the female character. When others joined in, they only talked. As they did not sing, they were known as supporting speakers. Singing was done by leading performers, and speakers only played a supporting role. By the time of the late Yuan and early Ming dynasties, however, this practice changed due to the influence of the Southern Opera, and all performers sang and they were no longer classified as leading or supporting roles. (Mao Qiling: *Mao Qiling's Remarks on Ci Poetry*)

bīngqiángzémiè 兵强则灭

Relying on Force and Flaunting One's Superiority Leads to Destruction.

倚仗武力逞强就会灭亡。这是中国古代哲学家老子"守柔"理念的具体体现。老子认为，任何事物都有刚与柔、强与弱两个方面，这两个方面不是绝对的，在一定条件下它们可以相互转化；而且，从长远看，貌似刚强的东西，其实已经达到自己的极限；貌似柔弱的东西，反而更富于生机活力，处于上升趋势。就像那些自恃武力而四处逞强的国家一样，最终都会走向自己的反面。它告诉我们，治理国家、处理人际关系，千万不要过分刚强，更不能恃强凌弱，要以柔克刚、柔中有刚、刚柔相济，这样才能实现稳定和谐的局面。

This is a concrete embodiment of ancient Chinese philosopher Laozi's concept of *shourou* (守 maintain; 柔 tenderness, gentleness). Laozi believed that every object has two sides, firmness as well as tenderness, strength as well as weakness. These two sides are not absolute, but under certain conditions, they can transform into the other. However, in the long run, things that appear to be firm and strong have in actuality reached its optimum, whereas things that are seemingly tender and weak are still full of vitality and vigor, and can escalate even further, just as those states which rely on force and flaunt their superiority everywhere will ultimately move towards their own destruction. This tells us that, in governing a state, or in managing interpersonal relations, one should never be overly staunch, and should not bully the weak. Instead, one should conquer the unyielding with gentleness, be firm but gentle, and tamper force with mercy, and only then can stability and harmony be achieved.

引例 Citation：

◎ 人之生也柔弱，其死也坚强。（万物）草木之生也柔脆，其死也枯槁。故坚强者死之徒，柔弱者生之徒。是以兵强则灭，木强则折。（《老子·七十六章》）

（人活着的时候身体是柔软的，死了以后身体就僵硬了。草木生长时是柔韧的，死了以后就干枯了。所以坚强的东西属于走向死亡的一类，柔弱的东西属于正在生长的一类。因此，依仗武力逞强就会灭亡，树木过于强硬就会折断。）

When a man is alive, his body is soft and weak. Upon his death, it becomes hard and stiff. When grass and trees live, they are soft and fragile. Upon their death, they turn withered and dry. Therefore, the hard and stiff are followers of death; the soft and weak are followers of life. That is why when an army flaunts its strength, it will soon perish, while when a tree becomes strong it snaps. (*Laozi*)

bóshī-jìzhòng 博施济众

Deliver Extensive Benefits to the People and Relieve the Suffering of the Poor

广泛地给予百姓好处并救济困苦的民众。"博施济众"是对为政者的一项很高的要求。"博施济众"的实现要求为政者以仁爱之心对待治下的百姓，体察百姓的需求与困苦，并在为政中广泛地施予好处、帮助。做到"博施济众"的为政者即具备了"圣"的德性。

Delivering a wide range of benefits to the people and relieving the suffering of the poor is crucial for good governance. It requires that a ruler must treat his subjects with benevolence, be responsive to people's needs and their difficulties and bring extensive benefits to them. Such a ruler deserves to be called a sage.

引例 Citation：

◎子贡曰："如有博施于民而能济众，何如？可谓仁乎？"子曰："何事于仁，必也圣乎！尧舜其犹病诸。"(《论语·雍也》)

（子贡问："如果有为政者做到广泛地给予百姓好处并救济困苦的民众，怎么样呢？可以称得上仁德吗？"孔子说："何止于仁德，那一定是圣德了！尧和舜都难以做到呢。"）

Zigong asked: "If a ruler delivers extensive benefits to his people and relieves the suffering of the poor, how would you rate him? Do you consider him benevolent and virtuous?" Confucius said: "He is far more than benevolent and virtuous.

I would call him a sage. Even virtuous rulers such as Yao and Shun could not match him." (*The Analects*)

bùyánzhījiào 不言之教

Influence Others Without Preaching

以不言说的方式施行的教化。这是老子提出的一种符合"无为"原则的教化方式。古代一般意义上的教化，是统治者通过言语表达的各种命令、训导，使百姓的言行乃至心灵符合礼法的要求。老子反对这种"有为"的教化方式，认为统治者不应按照自己的意志命令、训导百姓，而应以"无为""无言"的方式，因循、保全百姓的自然状态。后多用"不言之教"指以自身的品行来影响、引导他人。

Laozi advocated "influencing others without preaching" as part of his philosophy of *wuwei* (无为) or non-action. In ancient times, rulers issued orders and instructions to shape their subjects' speech, thoughts and behavior so as to conform to the proprieties. Laozi was against this kind of direct action, believing that instead of imposing their own will on the people, the sovereign should employ non-action and non-preaching methods to preserve and protect the natural state of their subjects. Later, the term came to mean influencing and guiding others by one's moral conduct.

引例 Citations：

◎是以圣人处无为之事，行不言之教。(《老子·二章》)

（因此圣人以无为的方式处理世事，以不言的方式教导百姓。）

Therefore, sages deal with the world's affairs by way of non-action, teach people without uttering a word. (*Laozi*)

◎不言之教，无为之益，天下希及之。(《老子·四十三章》)

("不言"的教化，"无为"的益处，天下很少有人能够做到。)

Few can truly teach others without preaching, and do good through non-action. (*Laozi*)

cángfùyúmín 藏富于民

Keep Wealth with the People

　　将财富贮存在民众手中。这是中国古已有之的政治经济思想，先秦时期儒、墨、道、法、兵等各个流派对此均有阐发。它要求为政者薄敛节用，不要与民争利，搜刮民财；另一方面对百姓要实行宽惠政策，允许、鼓励百姓合理谋利致富。其中隐含有关于民富与国富统一性的认识：民富是国富的基础，也是国家赢得民心的根本保障；而国富的根本不仅在于财富，更在于民心。它是"民本"思想的延伸。时至今日，藏富于民已成为现代文明的根本特征之一。

The concept of keeping wealth with the people has long been a part of Chinese political economy. Prior to the Qin Dynasty, the Confucian, Mohist, Daoist, and Legalist scholars as well as military strategists all expounded on this subject. A ruler is expected to be frugal and will not compete with the people for benefits, nor plunder their riches. Policies that are generous towards the people should be adopted, so as to permit and encourage them to become rich through justified means. The underlying assumption here is that a wealthy populace and a wealthy state are one and the same. A wealthy populace is the foundation of a state's wealth as well as the fundamental guarantee for the state to win popular support. A state's wealth is more than just about its riches, but about people's support as well. This is an extension of the concept of "putting the people first," and in the present day, keeping wealth with the people has become a defining feature of modern civilization.

引例 Citations：

◎善为国者，必先富民，然后治之。(《管子·治国》)
（善于治理国家的人，一定会将使百姓富裕放在首位，然后才考虑如何治理百姓。）

A person good at governing a state will always first enrich his people before considering their governance. (*Guanzi*)

◎取于民有度，用之有止，国虽小必安；取于民无度，用之不止，国虽大必危。(《管子·权修》)
（对人民征收赋税有限度，使用上也有节制，国家即使小但一定能安定；若对人民征收赋税没有限度，使用上也不加以节制，国家即使大也一定会有危险。）

If there are limits to taxes levied on the people and the use of such taxes is under control, a state will enjoy stability even if it is small. If there are no limits to the taxes levied on the people and there is no control on how such taxes are spent, a state will face peril even if it is large. (*Guanzi*)

◎善为国者，藏之于民。(《三国志·魏书·赵俨传》)
（善于治理国家的人，让民众拥有、存储财富。）

A ruler good at governing a state will let his people keep their wealth. (*The History of the Three Kingdoms*)

chéngzhúyúxiōng 成竹于胸

Have a Complete Image of the Bamboo Before Drawing It / Have a Fully Formed Picture in the Mind's Eye

在文艺创作开始前，艺术形象已在头脑中生成。这一术语揭示了文艺创作运用形象思维的特点，也是对文艺创作乃至工艺设计提出的要求。对于文艺创作者来说，思想观念、情感、意志与物象结合，在心中形成审美意象，艺术构思已经完成，然后才是运用技巧、借助物质材料外化为具体可感的作品。对于工艺设计者来说，则有更多的理性思考，允许修改，而成竹在胸则是一种理想状态。

This term means to have an image of the art in one's mind prior to artistic creation. It describes the use of mental imagery in the course of artistic creation, and also sets a requirement for both artistic creation and for design in craftsmanship. For the creator of an artwork, concepts, feelings, intentions and objects should be integrated in the mind to form an aesthetic image. After this artistic conceptualization is completed, technique is used in conjunction with physical materials to form a tangible work. For a craft designer, the emphasis would be more on rational thinking, and revisions would be permissible. Having a fully formed picture in advance is an ideal state.

引例 Citations：

◎故画竹必先得成竹于胸中，执笔熟视，乃见其所欲画者，急起从之，振笔直遂，以追其所见，如兔起鹘落，少纵则逝矣。（苏轼《文与可画筼筜谷偃

竹记》）

（所以说画竹一定要先在心中生成竹子的整体形象，拿着画笔仔细观察竹子，然后才可能在心中出现所想要画的竹子，这时要急速起身追赶这一形象，挥笔作画，一气呵成，捕捉住心中所想的竹子，就像兔子跃起、鹰隼俯冲一样迅速，稍一放松，竹子的形象就消失了。）

Thus when drawing bamboo, you must first have a complete image of the bamboo in your mind's eye. First hold the pen while carefully observing the bamboo; only then will the bamboo you wish to draw appear in your mind's eye. Then, as quickly as a leaping hare or a swooping raptor, you must wield your pen and capture this image in one go. The slightest letup and the image of the bamboo will be lost. (Su Shi: An Essay on Wen Yuke's Drawing "The Valley of Bamboos")

◎文与可画竹，胸有成竹；郑板桥画竹，胸无成竹。浓淡疏密，短长肥瘦，随手写去，自尔成局，其神理具足也。（郑板桥《板桥题画·竹》）

（文与可画竹，心里先有竹子的完整形象；郑板桥画竹，心中没有竹子的完整形象。竹子颜色是浓是淡，枝叶是疏是密，竹身是短是长、是肥是瘦，都是随手而画，自成一种形态，也都充分表现出了竹子的纹理神韵。）

When Wen Yuke draws bamboo, he already has a complete image of the bamboo in his mind. When Zheng Banqiao draws bamboo, he does not have a complete image of the bamboo in his mind. The colors of his bamboo might be dark or pale; the leaves might be dense or sparse, the stems might be short or long, thick or slender – they are all drawn spontaneously, assuming a form of their own and fully displaying their own textures and charms. (Zheng Banqiao: *Banqiao's Calligraphies in Paintings*)

chuánshén-xiězhào 传神写照

Convey the Spirit and Capture the Person

指文学艺术作品中所描绘或刻画的人物生动逼真、形神兼备。"传神"是将人物内在的精神世界完全表现出来，使人物栩栩如生；"写照"就是画像，所绘人物形象逼真，如在目前。初为画论术语，后引入文学领域，是画家、文学家在塑造人物形象及一切艺术形象时所追求的艺术境界。

This term refers to literary descriptions of characters which are accurate both in form and in spirit. *Chuanshen* (传神), to "convey the spirit," is to fully express the spiritual world within the character, so that he comes to life; *xiezhao* (写照), to "capture the person," is to create a vivid physical depiction of him. These expressions were originally used in discussions of art but were later introduced into literature. They represent an artistic state which artists and writers try to achieve as they create images of people as well as all artistic images.

引例 Citations：

◎四体妍蚩（chī），本无关于妙处，传神写照，正在阿堵中。（刘义庆《世说新语·巧艺》）
（人物形象的美丑，本来显现不出画作的高妙之处；真正能够让人物形神兼备、生动鲜活起来的地方，就是那个眼睛。）

The heights of artistry do not lie in whether or not someone's physical shape is well portrayed. Rather, it is the eyes which convey the spirit and capture the person. (Liu Yiqing: *A New Account of Tales of the World*)

◎空中荡漾最是词家妙诀。上意本可接入下意，却偏不入。而于其间传神写照，

乃愈使下意栩栩欲动。（刘熙载《艺概·词概》）

（在本应接着抒情表意的地方故意转写他事从而留出意义上的空白，是填词高手的妙诀。抒情表意本可前后相接，但作者偏偏没有接写反而转向其他的描写或叙事，通过空白愈发将人物的内心活动鲜活地传达出来，使得接下来的抒情表意更为鲜明灵动、栩栩如生。）

It is a subtle trick of great lyric writers to deliberately change the subject or to leave something unsaid. Where one thought can give rise to another, the author deliberately refrains from doing so, and instead turns to other descriptions or narratives, thus creating a void which conveys the spirit and captures the person. By doing so, lyrical expression becomes even more vivid and lifelike. (Liu Xizai: *Overview of Literary Theories*)

◎描画鲁智深，千古若活，真是传神写照妙手。（李贽《李卓吾先生批评忠义水浒传》）

（作者所刻画的鲁智深，即使千年以后也还活在人们眼前，真是善于传神写照的高手啊！）

The image of Lu Zhishen portrayed by the author remains lifelike even after a thousand years. He is truly a master who can convey the spirit and capture the person! (Li Zhi: *Li Zhi's Annotations on Outlaws of the Marsh*)

chūnjié 春节

Spring Festival

中华民族及海外华人最重要的传统节日。狭义的春节指农历新年第一个月的第一天，广义的春节是指从农历最后一个月的 23 日（祭灶）到新年第一个月的 15 日（元宵节）这一段时间。现代意义的春节实际上是古代一年之始与立春节气两者的混合。春节期间，人们会祭拜神灵和祖先，张贴春联和年画，置办年货，吃团圆饭，给压岁钱，除夕守岁，燃放爆竹，走亲访友，等等。它凝结着中国人的伦理情感、宗教情怀、生命意识，具有深厚的历史内涵和丰富的节俗内容。在伦理与宗教层面，除了祭祀，祈求祖先和神灵对家人的庇佑，春节更多体现了中国人对家族团圆、和睦及亲情的重视；在时间与生命意识上，在辞旧迎新、驱除邪祟的同时，表达人们对新年的祝福及对未来生活的美好期待。受中华文化影响，中国周边一些国家和民族也有庆祝春节的习俗。

This is the most important traditional festival for the Chinese nation and overseas Chinese. In the narrow sense, it is the first day of the Lunar New Year. In a broader sense, it refers to the festival that occurs between the 23rd day of the last lunar month (the day of Offerings to the Kitchen God) and the 15th day of the first lunar month (the Lantern Festival). In a modern sense, Spring Festival is a mixture of the beginning of the New Year and the Beginning of Spring on the lunar calendar. During the Spring Festival, people pay tribute to deities and their ancestors, post auspicious couplets and New Year paintings, buy new year's goods and put on new clothes, have a family reunion dinner, give children gift money, stay up the whole night on New Year's Eve to say goodbye to the departing year, set off firecrackers and visit relatives and friends. In terms of family relationships and religion, people make sacrifices to ancestors and deities for the protection of their family members. In addition, Spring Festival reflects the importance Chinese people attach to family reunion, harmony within a family and kinship. When it comes to the Chinese people's sense of life and sense of time, they not only bid farewell to the departing year and express their welcome to the new year, they also express their expectation for a better future. Through the influence of Chinese culture, some of China's neighboring countries also celebrate Spring Festival.

引例 Citation：

◎爆竹声中一岁除，春风送暖入屠苏。千门万户曈（tóng）曈日，总把新桃换旧符。(王安石《元日》)

（爆竹声中，旧的一年缓缓离去；春风送来温暖，全家人聚在一起品尝着屠苏美酒。太阳升起，朝霞照亮了千门万户；为了除旧迎新，家家争先恐后地换上新的桃符。）

The year departs amid the sound of fireworks, and a warm breeze helps to ferment the wine. When the light of dawn shines upon thousands of homes, every family puts up New Year couplets. (Wang Anshi: New Year's Day)

dàxué 大学

Daxue (Great Learning)

人们在不同意义上使用"大学"的概念。其一，从学校制度而言，"大学"指由国家设立的最高等级的学校，即"太学"，有别于地方设立的"塾""庠（xiáng）""序"等。其二，从教学内容而言，"大学"即所谓成人之学，主要讲授为人处事、治国理政的道理与原则，有别于学习文字或具体礼仪、技艺的"小学"。其三，从教学目标而言，"大学"旨在帮助学生确立健全的人格与德性，培养治国理政的人才。

The concept means different things in different contexts. In terms of institutions of learning, it refers to the institution of highest learning, the imperial academy, established by the state, which is different from local schools. When it comes to content of learning, it refers to what a complete man should learn, namely, general rules and principles on governance and human relationship, which are different from that of *xiaoxue* (小学 little learning), namely, learning of words and specific rites or skills. In terms of objective, great learning aims to help students develop sound personality and moral integrity and thus make them qualified for exercising governance.

引例 Citations：

◎古之教者，家有塾，党有庠（xiáng），术（suì）有序，国有学。比年入学，中年考校。一年视离经辨志，三年视敬业乐群，五年视博习亲师，七年视论学取友，谓之小成。九年知类通达，强立而不反，谓之大成。夫然后足以化民易俗，近者说（yuè）服，而远者怀之，此大学之道也。(《礼记·学记》)

（古代的教育，家族中设有塾，每一党设有庠，每一遂设有序，诸侯国的国都设有学。学生每年入学，隔年考核。第一年考察经文断句、理解经典的能力及学习志向，第三年考察是否专注学业、友爱同学，第五年考察是否博学、亲爱老师，第七年考察学问上是否有独立见解和选取良友的能力，称为小成。第九年考察是否能够触类旁通、通达无碍，坚定独立而不违反所学的道理，称为大成。如此之后足以教化民众、改易风俗，附近的民众都对他心悦诚服，而远方的民众也都来归附他，这就是大学教育的步骤和目标。）

The educational system in ancient times consisted of small schools for each clan in a village, higher level schools for every 500 households, even higher level schools for every 12,500 households and institutions of higher learning at the capital of a ducal state. Students were enrolled every year, and examinations were held every other year. During the first year, students learned how to punctuate classics and studied them, and they developed motivation through learning. By the third year, students should immerse themselves in learning and develop fraternity with fellow students. During the fifth year, students should gain comprehensive knowledge and hold their teachers in reverence. In the seventh year, students should learn enough to form independent judgment and they should make true friends, which was called secondary attainment. In the ninth year, they should gain a keen sense of what connects different things, have self-confidence, and be independent in thinking without going against what they've learned. This was called great attainment. A scholar trained this way could educate others and improve social mores, and thus enjoyed the respect of people both near and afar. This is what great learning should achieve. (*The Book of Rites*)

◎大学之道，在明明德，在亲民，在止于至善。(《礼记·大学》)

（大学的宗旨，在于彰显光明的德性，在于亲和民众，在于达到言行的至善。）

Great learning aims to foster moral integrity, forge close ties with the people and attain consummate virtue in both words and deeds. (*The Book of Rites*)

duótāi-huàngǔ 夺胎换骨

Express the Ideas in Earlier Literary Works in a New Way

原意为脱去凡胎俗骨而换为圣胎仙骨，后比喻在诗文创作中援用前人作品的意思但能用自己的语言另立新意的一种技法。强调师法前人而不露痕迹并能有所创新。在诗歌创作中主要通过换字、换意凸显主旨、生成新意、造就佳句。"夺胎"是发现前人作品中具有某种意味，而予以阐扬、深化、拓展，乃至生成新意。"换骨"是发现前人作品中具有某种高妙的思想、情意但表现不够充分，而用更为恰切的语言予以重新表现，使之更完善、更鲜明。这一技巧体现文艺创作的传承、流变关系，在作品中可以看到很多具体运用的实例。文化学术的继承和发展也可以借鉴这一策略。

This term, which figuratively means to replace the flesh and bones of an ordinary human being with those of an immortal, is used to describe a literary technique in which a writer uses his own words to express new ideas while quoting those from earlier works. The emphasis is on borrowing from the past without showing any traces, yet forming something new in the process. In poetry, this is achieved primarily by substituting words and ideas to highlight a theme, thus creating a beautiful new phrase. *Duotai* (夺胎) is to identify an idea in an existing work and to imbue it with new meaning by expounding, deepening or broadening it. *Huangu* (换骨) is to identify a brilliant idea or feeling in an earlier work which is insufficiently expressed, and to give it greater refinement and clarity by expressing it with a more appropriate choice of words. This technique exemplifies how literature both perpetuates and yet changes tradition. Cultural scholarship can also borrow from this method to build on the past and to further develop.

引例 Citations：

◎然不易其意而造其语，谓之换骨法；窥入其意而形容之，谓之夺胎法。（释惠洪《冷斋夜话》卷一）

（然而不改变前人的意思而换用更恰切的词句，叫做换骨法；从前人作品中领悟到作者的某个意旨而予以深化和充分发挥，叫做夺胎法。）

Huangu is to use more appropriate words without changing the meaning of earlier writers; *Duotai* is to comprehend a certain meaning of an author and then deepen it and express it more fully. (Shi Huihong: *Evening Talks at Lengzhai*)

◎文章虽不要蹈袭古人一言一句，然古人自有夺胎换骨等法，所谓灵丹一粒点铁成金也。（陈善《扪虱新话·文章夺胎换骨》）

（文章虽然不应该袭用前人的一字一句，但前人自有一种夺胎换骨的方法，就好像用一粒灵丹来点铁成金［从而创造出更完美的作品］一样。）

Though not copying earlier writings word from word, the ancients had a way of "replacing the flesh and bones" which, like a magic pill turning iron into gold, brings forward even better works. (Chen Shan: *Daring Remarks on Literature*)

fǎ yǔ shí biàn, lǐ yǔ sú huà 法与时变，礼与俗化

Laws Change Along with Evolving Times; Rites Shift Along with Changing Customs.

国家的制度和法令随时代而改变，社会的礼义随风俗而变化。法：既指制度和律法，还包括由统治者颁布的各种政令。时：指时代、时势。礼：主要指社会的道德规范和行为准则。俗：除了习俗、风气，还包括国情民意。它认为一切都是变化发展的，制度、法令与礼义也应随着时代的发展而做出相应的调整。它反对因循守旧，主张创新变革，一切以顺应时势和国情民意为治国理政的根本原则。它是《周易》"与时偕行"这一思想的发挥，也蕴含儒家所倡导的"民本"思想。

In the context of this term, "laws" refer to the administrative edicts of a ruler as well as institutions and laws. "Times" refer primarily to the prevailing social conditions. "Rites" mainly refer to a society's moral norms and codes of conduct. In addition to social conventions and mores, "customs" also include popular sentiment. This expression means since everything is constantly changing and evolving, institutions, laws and rites must change correspondingly. It opposes being bound by tradition, favors innovation and change, and espouses the basic principle that a country's governance should follow the times and respond to popular will. This is an example of the concept of "going with the times" contained in *The Book of Changes*, and it also resonates with the concept of "putting the people first" advocated by Confucianism.

引例 Citations：

◎故古之所谓明君者，非一君也，其设赏有薄有厚，其立禁有轻有重，迹行不必同，非故相反也，皆随时而变，因俗而动。(《管子·正世》)

（因此古时所谓贤明君王，不只是一人，他们设立的赏赐有多有少，颁布的禁令有轻有重。他们的做法不必完全一样，但也不是故意使之不同，都是随时代的发展而改变，随风俗的变化而改变。）

Hence there was more than one so-called wise ruler in ancient times. They gave out rewards which varied from big and small, their proscriptions might be harsh or light and their methods were not always the same. This is not because they were deliberately trying to be different, but because they changed with the evolving times and shifted as customs changed. (*Guanzi*)

◎圣人者，明于治乱之道，习于人事之终始者也。其治人民也，期于利民而止。故其位齐也，不慕古，不留今，与时变，与俗化。(《管子·正世》)

（圣人都是懂得国家安定与动乱的规律、熟悉人情事理变化的人。他们治理民众，只希望对民众有利就可以了。所以他们确立适中的原则，不仰慕古人，也不拘泥于当今，而是根据时势而变迁、随着风气而改变。）

A sage is someone who knows what causes a state to enjoy stability or fall into turmoil, someone who is aware of changing customs. When a sage rules, he hopes only to do what is good for his people. Thus he establishes appropriate principles, neither worshipping the past nor allowing himself to be bound by the present. He changes along with the evolving times and shifts along with changing customs. (*Guanzi*)

◎故圣人法与时变，礼与俗化。衣服器械，各便其用；法度制令，各因其宜。(《文子·上义》)

(所以圣人[治理国家]，制度和法令随时代而改变，礼义随风俗而变化。衣服器械之类，都为了使用方便；法令制度，都根据实际情况制定合宜的办法。)

Thus when a sage rules, laws change with the evolving times and rites shift along with changing customs. Clothes and instruments are made to suit their uses, laws and edicts are adopted to meet actual needs. (*Wenzi*)

fǎnqiúzhūjǐ 反求诸己

Introspection

反省自己的言行与内心。"反求诸己"是孟子（前372？—前289）提出的一种道德修养方法。孟子秉承了儒家的主张，认为人的德行与功业的确立，从根本上取决于自身的修养。因此，如果自己的言语行事不能获得认可与赞赏，不应归咎于他人的误解，而应反省自己的言行与内心是否符合道德、礼法的要求。

This term refers to self-examination of one's own words, deeds, and inner thoughts. Introspection is a way of moral cultivation put forward by Mencius

(372?-289 BC). Mencius inherited the Confucian belief that one's moral integrity and meritorious deeds are determined by his own ethical cultivation. If his words or deeds fail to gain endorsement or appreciation from others, one should not blame them. On the contrary, one should examine himself to find out if his words and deeds as well as inner thoughts conform to standards of ethics and propriety.

引例 Citations：

◎仁者如射，射者正己而后发，发而不中，不怨胜己者，反求诸己而已矣。(《孟子·公孙丑上》)

（仁者就好比射箭的人一样，射箭的人要首先端正自己的姿势然后发箭，发箭没有射中目标，不埋怨成绩超过自己的人，而是反躬自省而已。）

A virtuous man is like an archer. The archer adjusts himself and then shoots. Should he miss, he is not jealous of those who defeat him. He simply examines himself to find out why he has not won. (*Mencius*)

◎爱人不亲，反其仁；治人不治，反其智；礼人不答，反其敬。行有不得者，皆反求诸己，其身正而天下归之。(《孟子·离娄上》)

（我爱别人而别人不亲爱我，则反省自己是否仁爱；我治理别人而没有治理好，则反省自己是否智慧；我以礼待人却没得到回应，则反省自己是否不恭敬。任何行为如果没有达到预期效果，都要反躬自省，自己立身端正则天下之人都会归附。）

If others do not reciprocate your kindness towards them, you should think about whether your kindness is true or not. If you govern unsuccessfully, think about whether your governance philosophy is sound or not. If others do not reciprocate your courtesy towards them, think about whether your courtesy is sincere or not. Whenever you fail to achieve the desired result, you need to conduct retrospection to find out the cause. If you conduct yourself honorably, all the people will pledge allegiance to your rule. (*Mencius*)

fēngròu-wēigǔ 丰肉微骨

Fleshy Body and Soft Bone Structure

原指女性身材娇小、肌肉丰腴而身段柔软，后用于书画品评，指运笔丰肥、媚浮而骨力纤弱。"骨"即骨法，指笔势或结构上的清劲雄健；"肉"指线条的丰肥、妍媚无力或浓墨重彩。古人强调书画创作应有骨有肉、骨肉匀称，既不失妍美而又雄健有力。因此，"丰肉微骨"是差评，而"丰骨微肉"或"骨丰肉润"则各有千秋。这一术语从人物的鉴赏延伸到艺术作品鉴赏，体现了中国美学概念"近取诸身"的特点。

Originally this term indicated that a woman had a delicate figure, that she was fleshy and limber. Later it was used to judge calligraphy and painting, indicating that the circulation of the writing brush was lavish and vigorous, but that the strength of the bone (structure) was weak. Bone (structure) means skeletal structure, indicating weakness or vigor in the strength of the writing brush and in the structure of the work. "Fleshy" indicates that the lines are sumptuous and charming, but without strength, or that the ink is thick and the colors heavy. In the old days, it was stressed that a work of calligraphy or a painting should have a bone (structure) and be fleshy and that there should be a proper balance between the bone and flesh. There should neither be a lack of elegance nor of vigor and strength. Therefore, "fleshy body and soft bone structure" is regarded as a demerit. But when there is a stout bone structure and soft muscles, or when the bone structure is stout and the muscles are smooth, both are considered desirable. This term shifted from depicting human figures to appreciating art works, giving expression to the Chinese aesthetic concept of "using body parts to describe what is near."

引例 Citations：

◎丰肉微骨，调以娱只。(《楚辞·大招》)

(身材娇小而丰腴柔美的女人哪，舞姿和谐令人欢快轻松。)

With delicate, fleshy and soft figures, the lady dancers delighted the audience with their performance. (*Odes of Chu*)

◎善笔力者多骨，不善笔力者多肉；多骨微肉者谓之筋书，多肉微骨者谓之墨猪；多力丰筋者圣，无力无筋者病。(卫夫人《笔阵图》)

(笔力强的人，其作品的筋骨多清劲雄健；而笔力弱的人，其作品则是多浓墨。骨法鲜明雄健而着墨少的字叫做"筋书"，用墨浓重而不见骨法的字叫做"墨猪"。筋骨饱满有力的作品最高妙，筋骨少而无力属于很差的作品。)

Those who are good at using the writing brush can create fresh and vigorous calligraphic pieces like a body with strong bone structure, whereas those who are not can only produce inky calligraphic pieces. A vigorous calligraphic work done without much ink is called "a sinewy work," while a less vigorous piece done with much ink is called "an inky piglet." A vigorous work is to be highly appreciated, while a less vigorous one is undesirable. (Lady Wei: On Maneuvers of Calligraphy)

gǎnwù 感物

Sensed Externalities

指人为外物所触动产生了创作冲动，经过构思与艺术加工，形成为文艺作品。"物"指直观可感的自然景物、生活场景。古人认为创作缘起于外界事物的感召而激起了创作欲望，文艺作品是外物与主观相结合的产物。这一术语强调了文艺创作源于生活的基本理念。

A person's creative impulse is triggered by one or more externalities, and after conceptualization and artistic treatment, this results in a work of art. Such externalities include both natural sights and scenes from life which can be directly sensed. Ancient Chinese believed that creation resulted from externalities which evoked a desire to create, and that works of art and literature were the result of combining externalities with subjective thinking. This term emphasizes the fundamental idea that artistic creation is rooted in life.

引例 Citations：

◎凡音之起，由人心生也。人心之动，物使之然也。感于物而动，故形于声。(《礼记·乐记》)

(一切音乐都起源于人的内心。人的内心之所以产生活动，是受到外物感发的结果。人受外物的感发而产生内心活动，所以会通过音乐表达出来。)

All music originates in people's hearts. Feelings arise in people's hearts because externalities cause them to do so. Hearts are moved by externalities, hence they express themselves through music. (*The Book of Rites*)

◎人禀七情，应物斯感，感物吟志，莫非自然。(刘勰《文心雕龙·明诗》)

（人具有喜、怒、哀、惧、爱、恶、欲等七种情感，受到外物的刺激而心有所感，心有所感而吟咏情志，所有的诗歌都出于自然情感。）

People have the seven emotions of joy, anger, sadness, fear, love, loathing and desire. He expresses his feelings and aspirations in a poetical way when he is stimulated by the external world and his heart is touched. All poems come from natural emotions. (Liu Xie: *The Literary Mind and the Carving of Dragons*)

guāng'érbùyào 光而不耀

Bright but Not Dazzling

光明而不刺眼。老子用"光而不耀"来形容执政者对百姓的影响。在老子看来，执政者具有显赫的地位，并且掌握着足以影响百姓生活的权力与资源。从这个意义上来说，执政者对百姓的影响如同光照一样，是显明而不容回避的。但老子同时强调，执政者不应将自己的意志强加给百姓，而应因循、保全百姓的自然状态。百姓受到影响却不被伤害，如同在光明之中而不感到刺眼。"光而不耀"也可用于形容强者对待他人的方式。

This term means to be bright without being dazzling. Laozi used the term to describe the influence of those in power on ordinary people. High status, authority and resources enable them to have a great impact on people's lives, just like a bright light that cannot be avoided. However, Laozi also believed that no person in power should impose his will on the people, whose natural state should be maintained and protected. To be influenced but not harmed is like being surrounded by light but not dazzled by it. The term can be used to describe the way any powerful person should treat others.

引例 Citation：

◎是以圣人方而不割，廉而不害，直而不肆，光而不耀。(《老子·五十八章》)

（因此圣人方正而不割伤他人，清廉而不伤害他人，正直而不刺激他人，光明而不刺人眼目。）

The sage is ethical but not hurtful, incorruptible but not disdainful, candid but not offensive, bright but not dazzling. (*Laozi*)

hé tóngyì 合同异

Unify Similarity and Difference

把事物的同和异合而为一。"合同异"是惠施（前370？—前310？）提出的看待事物同异的一种方式。惠施认为，事物的同异是相对而言的。两个具体事物之间会有或大或小的相同或相异之处。从"同"的角度来看，万物有共同之处，因此可以说万物是相同的；而从"异"的角度来看，则没有完全相同的两个事物，万物是不同的。事物的同异取决于看待事物的角度，因此惠施主张打破同异的界限，也即是"合同异"。

The philosopher Hui Shi's (370?-310? BC) approach to similarity and difference among things was to unite them, regarding similarities and differences as relative. There are bound to be small or great similarities and differences between any two concrete things. If we look at them from the point of view of similarity, all things have something in common, so they can be said to be similar. If we look at them from the point of view of difference, no two things are completely the same, so they are all different. Whether things are similar or different depends on the perspective from which we look at them. This led Hui Shi to determine that similarities and differences are not separate; that is, they are unified.

引例 Citation：

◎大同而与小同异，此之谓"小同异"；万物毕同毕异，此之谓"大同异"。（《庄子·天下》）

（大同小异与小同大异是有区别的，这种区别称为"小同异"；万物完全相同、完全不同，这称为"大同异"。）

When there are major commonalities and minor differences, or minor commonalities and major differences, it is called "minor commonality and differentiation." When things are totally identical or totally different, it is called "major commonality and differentiation." (*Zhuangzi*)

hé chūyú shì 和出于适

Harmony Comes from Appropriateness.

音乐的和谐来自音乐的适度及音乐与平和心灵的契合。"和"，和谐，首先指不同声音之间的协调配合；"适"，适度，既指音乐本身高低、清浊的适度，亦指欣赏者对于音乐对象的适度接受。这一术语突出了音乐欣赏过程中作为客观对象的音乐必须与主体心灵的和谐相一致，音乐美感是主客体和谐的产物。

The harmony of music comes from its appropriateness and its concordance with the soul. "Harmony" refers to how different sounds are combined and attuned to each other. "Appropriateness" refers to the pitch and timbre of the music itself, as well as to the degree to which the listener can accept the music. This term highlights the need for harmony and accord between the object – music and the subject – the soul, in order for music to be appreciated. The beauty of music is generated by harmony between the subjective and the objective.

引例 Citation：

◎声出于和，和出于适。（《吕氏春秋·大乐》）

（音乐产生于不同声音的协调配合，而和谐须与欣赏者的心灵和谐相一致。）

Music comes from harmony, and harmony comes from appropriateness. (*Master Lü's Spring and Autumn Annals*)

hòujī-bófā 厚积薄发

Build Up Fully and Release Sparingly

充分地积累，少量地释放。多指学术研究或文艺创作等先要广泛汲取前人已有的知识和成果，待有了深厚的积累和坚实的基础，再一点儿一点儿地从事学术研究或文艺创作，尝试提出独到见解或在前人的基础上有所创造。也指一个国家、一个企业在某一领域或某一方面经过长期的积累，开始逐步展现其实力、创新力及开拓新的局面等。其核心内涵是，凡事不可急于求成，应注重积累，充分准备，才能把事情做好。

The term means to accumulate as much as possible but to release a little at a time. This often refers to the process of scholarly research or artistic creation, in which one should first extensively absorb the knowledge and results of others to acquire a wealth of knowledge and lay a solid foundation. On this basis, one is engaged in further scholarly studies or artistic creation, attempting to make new accomplishments. It can also refer to a country or a business which, after a long period of building up its strength, begins to gradually unleash its potential and ability to innovate and proceed to break new ground. The message of this expression is that one should never seek quick results; rather, one should pay attention to accumulating knowledge and making full preparations before making advances.

引例 Citation：

◎博观而约取，厚积而薄发，吾告子止于此矣。（苏轼《稼说——送张琥》）（读书要广博，吸取其精要；学问积累要深厚，慢慢释放出来。我能告诉你的就是这些了。）

Read widely and absorb the best from the books you read; acquire deep learning and share it gradually – that is all I can tell you. (Su Shi: An Allegory for Zhang Hu on Growing Crops)

huàxìng-qǐwěi 化性起伪

Transform Intrinsic Evil Nature to Develop Acquired Nature of Goodness

改变人的本性的恶而兴起人为的善。伪：人为。"化性起伪"是荀子（前313？—前238）在"性恶"论基础上提出的一种道德教化的主张。荀子认为，人天生的本性中包含着对外物的欲求。如果放纵本性中的欲望，就会导致人与人之间的纷争，社会将陷入混乱。因此，需要通过后天的教化，在恰当安顿人的欲望的同时，确立起对道德、礼法的认同与遵守。

This term means changing element of evil in one's intrinsic nature and developing acquired nature of goodness. This ethical principle is put forward by Xunzi (313?-238 BC) based on his belief that human nature is evil. Xunzi believes that the desire for external things is an intrinsic part of human nature. Unrestrained pursuit of such desire leads to rivalry between people and throws society into chaos. Therefore, it is imperative to rein in human desire and make people accept and observe rites and laws.

引例 Citations：

◎不可学、不可事而在人者谓之性，可学而能、可事而成之在人者谓之伪，是性、伪之分也。(《荀子·性恶》)
（不可以通过学习、从事而为人所具备的，称之为"性"；可以通过学习、从事而为人所具备的，称之为"伪"，这是"性"和"伪"的分别。）

Attributes that people have and that cannot be gained by learning and practice are called intrinsic nature. Abilities learned or mastered through practice are called acquired nature. Such is the difference between intrinsic nature and acquired nature. (*Xunzi*)

◎故圣人化性而起伪，伪起而生礼义，礼义生而制法度。(《荀子·性恶》)
（因此圣人改变人的本性的恶而兴起人为的善，人为的善兴起而产生了礼义，礼义产生而后制定法度。）

Thus, what the sage does is to transform the evil element in people's intrinsic nature and develop acquired nature of goodness. The acquired nature of goodness gives rise to rites and ethical standards, which in turn give birth to laws. (*Xunzi*)

huàn zhōng yǒu zhēn 幻中有真

Truth in Imagination

指文艺作品的情节与景象虽是通过想象与虚构写成但却具有内在的真实，可以折射社会现实。佛教与道家思想认为，现实社会是变幻不定的，人们不可执迷于这种幻象，而应当超越这种幻象，认识事物的真谛。文艺批评家提出，人们认识文艺作品与生活现实，应当善于透过幻象而把握作品的真实，获取美感。"幻中有真"作为一个文学批评术语，不仅揭示了文艺的审美特征和意义，也揭示了文艺创作的基本规律，即艺术形象的创造须以现实生活为依据，但又不能拘泥于现实生活，而应达到生活真实与艺术真实的高度统一。

The term means that the plot of scenes in a literary work, while imaginary, nonetheless have inner force and reflect reality in society. According to Buddhist and Daoist thought, society is transitory and shifting and people should not hold on to something unreal; rather, they should transcend delusions and recognise the true essence of things. As pointed out by literary and art critics, to gain keen appreciation of literary works and real life, people should learn to go beyond the imaginary aspect to grasp the truth of a creative work so as to enjoy its beauty. As a term in literary criticism, truth in imagination not only sheds light on the aesthetic function and significance of literature and arts, but also reveals a fundamental principle of literary and artistic creation, that is, art creation should be rooted in real life but not limited by it. Instead, it should aim at blending the truth of life and artistic imagination.

引例 Citations：

◎ 故不得已描写人生幻境之离合悲欢，以及善善恶恶，令阅者触目知警。（天花藏主人《〈幻中真〉序》）
（因此不得已通过虚构描写人生离合悲欢的情境，以及善得善报、恶得恶报的各种故事，让读者读到这些之后懂得警醒。）

Therefore, [the author] has to describe separation and reunion, happiness and sadness in the illusory world of human life, as well as telling stories of reward for good and punishment for evil deeds, so the reader learns from it and is warned. (Tianhuacangzhuren: Preface to *Truth in Imagination*)

◎ 即如《西游》一记……师弟四人各一性情，各一动止，试摘取其一言一事，遂使暗中摸索，亦知其出自何人，则正以幻中有真，乃为传神阿堵。（睡乡居士《二刻拍案惊奇》序）
（就拿《西游记》一书来说……师徒四人，各有各的性情，各有各的言行举止，尝试摘出某句话或某一举止，让人不看原书而暗自揣摩，也可以知道出自何人。正因为虚构的人物有现实的影子，才能够产生如见真人的传神效果。）

Take the novel *Journey to the West* as an example… The master and his three disciples each have their distinctive personalities, manners and behavior. If you cite a certain word or action and ask people to guess who did or said it, they will know who it is. Only when there is truth in imagination, can such a life-like effect be achieved. (Shuixiangjushi: Preface to *Amazing Stories, Vol. Two*)

huìhuà liù fǎ 绘画六法

Six Rules of Painting

中国古代关于绘画创作的六种手法与美学原则。南朝齐梁画家谢赫通过品鉴历代名家画作，总结出气韵生动、骨法用笔、应物象形、随类赋彩、经营位置、传移模写等六种基本方法与原则，初步建构起传统绘画理论体系。"气韵生动"是要求画作具有被观者真切感觉到的生气与神韵，是立足审美效果的总体原则。以下五方面是绘画的具体技法要求："骨法用笔"是指运笔能自如呈现人物的各种线条变化，"应物象形"是指造型要顺应对象的外形特征，"随类赋彩"是根据人物对象的特征进行着色，"经营位置"是指构图要合理搭配而呈现整体效果，"传移模写"是通过临摹佳作来掌握绘画技艺。后人据此品评画作，并就五方面技法要求展开论述、总结经验，丰富画论体系。"绘画六法"揭示了中国古代绘画的基本手法与美学原则，也是从事绘画批评的标准，它影响了六朝之后的中国绘画批评与创作实践。

The term refers to six techniques and aesthetic principles for painting formulated by Xie He, a painter between Qi and Liang of the Southern Dynasties. After studying famous painters of the previous age, he summarized his views on painting in six basic rules: dynamic style, forceful brush strokes, life-like image, characteristic coloring, careful arrangement and imitation and copying models. In this way, he established a theoretical framework for traditional painting. "Dynamic style" means that a painting should make the viewers appreciate its vitality and charm. This is a general principle focusing on the aesthetic effect. The other five rules concern specific techniques. "Forceful brush strokes" means being able to wield the brush to portray characters freely with lines of various shapes. "Life-like image" means the image should vividly capture the form of the depicted. "Characteristic coloring" means applying color according to the characteristics of the subject of the painting. "Careful arrangement" means a composition should achieve a good overall effect. "Imitation and copying models" means copying masterpieces to refine one's painting skills. These rules became the basis for later art criticism and discourse on the five aspects of technique, providing a summary of ideal painting techniques and enriching theory on painting. The "six rules of painting" cover the basic techniques and aesthetics of ancient Chinese painting. They also established guidelines for art appreciation and influenced criticism and artistic creation in China from the Six Dynasties on.

引例 Citations：

◎六法者何？一气韵生动是也，二骨法用笔是也，三应物象形是也，四随类赋彩是也，五经营位置是也，六传移模写是也。(谢赫《古画品录》)
(绘画的六个法则是什么呢？其一是作品要充满生气，富有神韵；其二是运笔能自如呈现各种线条变化；其三是造型要顺应对象外形特征；其四是要根据对象特征进行着色；其五是构图要合理搭配，呈现整体效果；其六是要临摹佳作以传承前人画技。)

There are six rules for painting. A painting should be full of vitality and artistic appeal; the painting brush should be used in such a way as to make changes in lines natural; image painted should suit the appearance of the painted object; coloring should suit the features of the object portrayed; the painting should be well structured to present an overall visual effect; and masterpieces of past painters should be copied to draw inspiration from them. (Xie He: *An Appraisal of Ancient Paintings*)

◎六法精论，万古不移，然而骨法用笔以下五法可学，如其气韵，必在生知，固不可以巧密得，复不可以岁月到，默契神会，不知然而然也。（郭若虚《画图见闻志·论气韵非师》）
（谢赫提出的绘画六法所论精当，万古不会改变。但是"骨法用笔"以下五方面可以学习，至于"气韵生动"，必定需要与生俱来的天赋，既不能凭借精巧细密而得到，也不能通过长期的积累获得，只能靠心灵去感悟、契合，虽不知怎么做但不知不觉就做到了。）

The six rules of painting are succinct and discerning and will stand the test of time. The latter five rules, starting with "forceful brush strokes," can be learned. But "dynamic style" requires innate aptitude and is not something that can be acquired just through scrupulous efforts or lengthy practice. Only an inspired mind can achieve dynamic style, yet without consciously knowing how. (Guo Ruoxu: *Experiences in Painting*)

huì shì hòu sù 绘事后素

The White Silk First, the Painting Afterwards / Beauty from Natural Simplicity

原指绘画须先有白绢作底，引申为美感源于自然质朴。孔子（前551—前479）由此阐发仁义为本、礼教为辅的理念，强调礼的教育起源于人的自然本性。后来这一术语引入文艺创作与批评，它倡导雕饰起源于质素，文质相符，彰显天然之美。

The original meaning of this phrase is that a piece of white silk must be prepared before one can paint. The concept was then extended to mean that beauty comes from natural simplicity. From this, Confucius (551-479 BC) put forward the notion that benevolence and righteousness are fundamental and the code of ethics secondary, emphasizing that the teaching of the rites originates in human nature. This concept was later introduced into literary and artistic creation and criticism, which advocates that elaboration should be based on substance, and that style and substance should be compatible and complement each other to bring out the natural beauty.

引例 Citations：

◎子夏问曰："'巧笑倩兮，美目盼兮，素以为绚兮。'何谓也？"子曰："绘事后素。"(《论语·八佾》)

（子夏问道："'美妙的笑靥那样迷人啊，漂亮的眼睛含羞顾盼啊，就像是白绢上画出了绚丽的画啊！'这几句诗是什么意思？"孔子道："先有白绢才能作画。"）

Zixia asked: "A seductive smile with pretty dimples, her lovely eyes sparkling, like a beautiful painting on white silk. What do these lines mean?" Confucius replied: "To paint, one must have a piece of white silk first." (*The Analects*)

◎礼必以忠信为质，犹绘事必以粉素为先。(朱熹《论语集注》卷二)

（礼教必须以忠信为根本，如同绘画必须先要有白绢。）

The ethical code must be based on loyalty and faithfulness, like a painting that must be done on a piece of white silk prepared. (Zhu Xi: *The Analects Variorum*)

jīshàn-chéngdé 积善成德

Moral Character Can Be Built by Accumulating Goodness.

积累善行以养成德性。"积善成德"是荀子（前313？—前238）所提出的一种德性养成方式。荀子认为，仅仅依循于人的本性，只能导致对外物无休止的争夺，并使群体陷入无秩序的混乱之中。而人的道德的确立有赖于后天的教化。人需要在言行表现上符合礼法的要求，并经过长期的积累，逐渐形成对道德、礼法的认同，确立起内在的道德意识。

Xunzi (313?-238 BC) first proposed this idea as a way to cultivate rectitude. He believed that following human nature alone leads to endless contention over external objects, resulting in disruption and discord within communities. Ethics and morals are instilled in a person through nurture and education. By conforming to the demands of proper speech and conduct over a long period of time, a person gradually develops a sense of propriety and inner morality.

引例 Citation：

◎积土成山，风雨兴焉；积水成渊，蛟龙生焉；积善成德，而神明自得，圣心备焉。（《荀子·劝学》）

（土堆积起来形成高山，风雨在这里产生。水积聚起来形成深渊，蛟龙在这里生长。善行不断积累以养成德性，就自然获得智慧，圣人的心智就具备了。）

Heaped earth makes mountains where wind and rain are born; water pools into deep lakes where dragons dwell; many good deeds build moral character that creates discernment, and prepare for the heart and mind of a sage. (*Xunzi*)

jísī-guǎngyì 集思广益

Pool Wisdom of the People

指汇集众人的思考与智慧,广泛吸取有益意见,以获得更好的效果。由三国时期的诸葛亮(181—234)提出。它要求领导者一定要广开言路,虚心听取各方意见,特别是那些与自己政见不合的意见,综合考虑,正确决策,绝不能自以为是、专断独行。这不仅是汇集智慧的过程,也是调动众人积极性、达成行动一致性的过程。

This means to work more effectively by extensively drawing on ideas and wisdom from many people. Proposed by Zhuge Liang (181-234) during the period of the Three Kingdoms, it meant that a leader should offer many opportunities for others to speak up and listen humbly to all opinions, especially those which differ from his own. He should then consider all aspects of the issue and make a correct decision. He absolutely must not think himself infallible and acts arbitrarily. Pulling wisdom of the people will keep everyone motivated and ensure success.

引例 Citations:

◎夫参署者,集众思广忠益也。(诸葛亮《与群下教》)
(但凡做官,就是要汇集众人的思考与智慧,广泛吸取忠直有益的意见。)

One who holds office should pool the ideas and wisdom of the people and extensively draw on all well intended and useful views. (Zhuge Liang: Instructions to Subjects and Officials)

◎故积力之所举,则无不胜也;众智之所为,则无不成也。(《淮南子·主术

训》)

(因此，聚合众人的力量托举某件物体，什么样的物体都能举起来；汇集众人的智慧去做某件事情，什么样的事情都能做成。)

Hence when the strength of many is brought together, there is nothing that cannot be lifted; when the wisdom of many is pooled, there is nothing that cannot be achieved. (*Huainanzi*)

jiǎngxìn-xiūmù 讲信修睦

Keep Good Faith and Pursue Harmony

崇尚诚信，谋求和睦。语出《礼记·礼运》。它是战国至秦汉之际儒家学者所描述的"大同"社会的重要特征之一。儒家认为最理想的社会应当是，天下是天下人的天下，人与人之间、国与国之间应彼此信任合作，和睦相处。后"讲信修睦"不仅成为儒家所提倡的一种伦理规范，而且成为中国文化中处理人际关系和国家关系的一个重要准则。

This term, from *The Book of Rites*, means attaching great value to good faith and seeking harmonious relations, which was a key feature of the society of "universal harmony" envisioned by Confucian scholars from the Warring States Period through the Qin and Han dynasties. They believed that in an ideal society, the land should belong to all its people, and there should be mutual trust, cooperation and harmonious relations between people and between states. "Keeping good faith and pursuing harmony" subsequently became an ethical norm advocated by Confucian scholars; it later also became an important Chinese cultural norm governing relations between people and between states.

引例 Citation：

◎大道之行也，天下为（wéi）公。选贤与能，讲信修睦。(《礼记·礼运》)
（大道实行的时代，天下为天下人所共有。品德高尚、才能突出的人被选拔出来管理社会，人与人之间讲求诚实与和睦。）

When the Great Way prevails, the world belongs to all the people. People of virtue and competence are chosen to govern the country; honesty is valued and people live in harmony. (*The Book of Rites*)

jiéqì 节气

The Twenty-four Solar Terms

二十四节气的简称，是中国传统农历中特有的现象。古人为了能更好地进行农事活动，从长期的农业实践中总结出了一套用于指导农耕的补充历法。根据太阳一年内在黄道的位置变化以及地面相应发生的气候、物候变化情况，把一年分成二十四段，每一段起始于一个节气，分列于十二个月，这就是二十四节气。二十四节气通常均匀分布于每月，月首的叫"节"，月中的叫"气"（每三年会出现有"节"无"气"或有"气"无"节"的情况，这时需设闰月进行调节）。节气的命名反映了季节、物候、气候三方面的变化。反映季节变化的是立春、春分、立夏、夏至、立秋、秋分、立冬、冬至八个节气；反映物候变化的是惊蛰、清明、小满、芒种四个节气；反映气候变化的有雨水、谷雨、小暑、大暑、处暑、白露、寒露、霜降、小雪、大雪、小寒、大寒十二个节气。二十四节气在秦汉时期就已形成，两千多年来，既有辅助农业生产的实际功效，也成为中国人所特有的时间观念。

"The twenty-four solar terms" is a unique phenomenon on the traditional lunar calendar. To facilitate agricultural production, ancient Chinese people summarized a supplementary calendar that divides a year into 24 segments according to the sun's movement on the ecliptic and seasonal changes in weather and other natural phenomena, with the 24 solar terms proportionally distributed through the 12 months. A solar term that starts in the early part of a month is called *jie* (节), and one that starts in the middle part of a month is called *qi* (气). (Every three years there would be a month which has only a *jie* without a *qi*, or a month which has only a *qi* without a *jie*, in which case a leap month would be added to regulate it.) The solar terms are so named that they represent the changes in season, phenology and climate. The eight solar terms that reflect seasonal changes are Beginning of Spring, Vernal Equinox, Beginning of Summer, Summer Solstice, Beginning of Autumn, Autumnal Equinox, Beginning of Winter, and Winter Solstice; the four solar terms that represent phenological changes are Waking of Insects, Fresh Green, Lesser Fullness, and Grain in Ear; and the 12 solar terms that indicate the changes in climate are Rain Water, Grain Rain, Lesser Heat, Greater Heat, End of Heat, White Dew, Cold Dew, First Frost, Light Snow, Heavy Snow, Lesser Cold, and Greater Cold. First established in the Qin and Han dynasties, the 24 solar periods have not only facilitated agricultural production but also reflected Chinese people's perception of time in the past more than two thousand years.

引例 Citation：

◎微雨众卉新，一雷惊蛰始。田家几日闲，耕种从此起。（韦应物《观田家》）

（绵绵细雨伴随百花清新，一声惊雷带来万物复苏。种田的人家哪有几日空闲，自此开始一年的耕种忙碌。）

Drizzles refresh all forms of greenery, / and thunder startles hibernators awake. / Farmers hardly have time to relax, / and tilling the soil starts now. (Wei Yingwu: Watching Farmers Working in Fields in Spring)

jìnzhōng-bàoguó 尽忠报国

Be as Loyal as One Can Be and Serve One's Own Country

竭尽忠诚，报效国家。亦作"精忠报国"。唐初编撰的《周书》《北史》已见"尽忠报国"一语。这一词语还与南宋抗金名将岳飞（1103—1142）相关联。元人所修《宋史》记载了岳飞后背刺有"尽忠报国"四字，但未说明何人所刺，至清代始有岳母刺字的说法，遂演绎为岳飞遵母命而尽忠报国、至死不渝的故事。它蕴含了忠孝合一的儒家理念，至今仍是中国人爱国精神的典型表达。

Be as loyal as one can be and serve one's own country. The term "be loyal and serve the country" first appeared in *The History of Zhou of the Northern Dynasties* and *The History of the Northern Dynasties* compiled during the early Tang. This phrase is also associated to the famous general in the war of resistance against the northern Jin invasion, Yue Fei (1103-1142) of the Southern Song Dynasty. In *The History of the Song Dynasty*, compiled during the Yuan Dynasty, there is a mention that Yue Fei had the four characters *jin zhong bao guo* (尽忠报国) tattooed on his back. However, it is not specified as to who tattooed them. Towards the Qing period, there were talks that it was Yue Fei's mother who tattooed them, and it is followed by the story of Yue Fei's commitment and obeisance to his mother's command to be loyal to his outmost and render service to his own country unto death. It has the connotation of Confucian ideals of loyalty and filial piety integrated into one, and to this day, it is used by the Chinese as a typical expression for patriotism.

引例 Citations：

◎公等备受朝恩，当思尽忠报国，奈何一旦欲以神器假人！（《周书·颜之仪传》）

（你们一直受朝廷重用厚待，就该想着怎么尽忠报国，为什么一天之内就打算将最高权力送给他人！）

You have always been highly placed and treated generously by the royal court, and hence you ought to be thinking ways to be the outmost loyal and render service to the country. Why is it then that you would consider giving away the highest power to others in just one day after you took hold of the power! (*The History of Zhou of the Northern Dynasties*)

◎［岳］飞袒而示之背，背有旧涅"尽忠报国"四大字，深入肤理。（《宋史·何铸传》）

（岳飞露出后背给何铸看，背上有先前刺的"尽忠报国"四个大字，已深入肌肤纹理中。）

Yue Fei exposed his back to show He Zhu the four characters *jin zhong bao guo* (尽忠报国 be as loyal as one can be and serve one's own country) which had been tattooed deep into the skin. (*The History of the Song Dynasty*)

jīng / quán 经 / 权

Constant and Temporary

中国哲学史上用来称说"道"的通常不变与权宜之变的一对哲学范畴。"经"是"道"在人伦日用中的通常表现，是通常应遵行的普遍之道，具有规范性的作用和意义。"权"的意思是从权、权变。在某些特殊处境中，按照"经"的规范行事会产生背离"道"的结果，这时就需要采取变通的方式，即"权"。"权"看似是对经常之"道"的偏离，但实质上是以权宜的方式合乎"道"的要求。在不同处境中对"经"与"权"的恰当选择与运用，取决于对"道"的深刻理解与把握。

Jing (经), which means the constant, and *quan* (权), which means the temporary, are terms used in the historical discourse of Chinese philosophy referring to a pair of philosophical concepts concerning the permanent and temporarily changing aspects of Dao. The constant is the normal manifestation of human relations and daily life. It is thus the normal way that should be observed. It has normative functions and significance. The temporary means a change of the function of Dao to suit circumstances or to meet needs of the day. In special circumstances, to follow the constant may result in deviation from Dao. When this happens, a flexible way, that is, the temporary, may be adopted. The temporary seems to deviate from Dao, but it actually conforms to requirements of Dao in a flexible manner. The application of the constant or the temporary in different circumstances is determined by one's keen understanding and mastery of Dao.

引例 Citations：

◎子曰："可与共学，未可与适道；可与适道，未可与立；可与立，未可与权。"
(《论语·子罕》)
(孔子说："可以与之共同学习的人，未必可以共同向道而行；可以与之共同向道而行的人，未必可以共同笃志不变；可以与之共同笃志不变的人，未必可以共同通权达变。")

Confucius said, "There are some whom you can join in study but whom you do not necessarily join in following the Dao. There are others whom you can join in following the Dao, but with whom you may not always share the same belief. There are still others with whom you may share the same belief, but whom you cannot join in applying flexibility as needed when following the Dao." (*The Analects*)

◎经者，道之常也；权者，道之变也。道是个统体，贯乎经与权。(《朱子语类》卷三十七)
(经是道的通常表现，权是对道的变通应用。道是一个统一体，贯穿于经与权的具体表现之中。)

The constant is a general expression of the Dao, while the temporary is a flexible application of the Dao. Dao unifies both the constant and the temporary. (*Categorized Conversations of Master Zhu Xi*)

jūnzǐ-gùqióng 君子固穷

A Man of Virtue Maintains His Ideals Even in Frustrations.

君子在困境中也能坚守道义。"君子"本指贵族男子和统治者，后泛指有教养、有德行的人；"固穷"即在穷困或在不得志的情况下，仍会坚持自己的理想、价值和操守。古人认为，困境是对"君子"的一种考验与历练，而"君子"在困境面前不会动摇本心，更不会失去底线。"君子固穷"犹言"安贫乐道""穷不失义"，它强调的是政治和文化精英的道义担当精神、社会引领责任。

Even under pressure, a man of virtue maintains his moral values. *Junzi* or man of virtue originally referred to a ruler or a man of the aristocracy. Later, it came to mean any educated, upright person. *Guqiong* (固穷) means to adhere to one's ideals and values even in times of difficulties and frustrations. The ancients believed that frustrated situations were ordeals for a man of virtue, in which he would not falter in his quest or touch the bottom line. This term summarizes the values of leadership, responsibility and integrity the political and cultural elites should retain in the face of difficulties and hardships.

引例 Citation：

◎子曰："君子固穷，小人穷斯滥矣。"(《论语·卫灵公》)
(孔子说："君子处于困境也能坚守道义，小人遇到困境就会不择手段了。")

Confucius said, "A man of virtue will uphold his ideals even in frustrations, but a petty man will stop at nothing." (*The Analects*)

kēzhèng měng yú hǔ 苛政猛于虎

Tyranny Is Fiercer than a Tiger.

苛刻残暴的政令比老虎还要凶猛可怕。语出《礼记·檀弓下》。孔子

（前551—前479）路过泰山脚下，有位妇女在墓前痛哭，孔子派子路（前542—前480）上前询问，得知当地虎患严重，她的三位亲人皆被老虎咬死，她却因这里没有苛政而不愿离开，故而孔子发出"苛政猛于虎也"的感叹。它从反面批评了苛政对百姓的祸害，告诫统治者应当轻徭薄赋、爱惜民众，体现了儒家的仁政思想。

Harsh and cruel laws are more horrifying even than a tiger. The expression comes from *The Book of Rites*. The story goes that when Confucius (551-479 BC) was passing the foot of Mount Tai, he saw a woman weeping on a grave. He sent Zilu (542-480 BC) over to inquire. The woman said there were many tigers in the area and that she had lost three of her family to them, but because the local laws were not harsh, she did not wish to move away. Confucius sighed and said, "Tyranny is fiercer even than a tiger." This is a criticism of harsh government, and an exhortation to rulers to reduce taxes and cut conscript labor, and to treat their subjects with compassion. It is an expression of Confucian principles of benevolent rule.

引例 Citation：

◎夫子曰："小子识（zhì）之，苛政猛于虎也。"（《礼记·檀弓下》）
（孔子说："年轻人要记住这件事，苛刻残暴的政令比老虎还要凶猛可怕呀！"）

Confucius says, "Remember this, young man, harsh and tyrannical laws are worse even than a fierce tiger." (*The Book of Rites*)

kǔyín 苦吟

Painstaking Versification

指唐代诗人贾岛（779—843）创作时苦思冥想、反复吟哦的创作方法。苦吟诗人多困顿失意，所以苦吟也被视为诗人借诗解愁的一种方式。有时也指从事文艺创作时精益求精的创作态度。

The Tang-dynasty poet Jia Dao (779-843) found composing his poems quite a painful process, and his creative method was to chant his verses repeatedly to get the right line. Those engaged in "painstaking versification" tended to be exhausted and frustrated, and their poetry is regarded as a way of relief for their sorrows. Sometimes, the term also refers to a perfectionist attitude to literary and artistic creation.

引例 Citations：

◎二句三年得，一吟双泪流。(贾岛《题诗后》)
(两句好诗三年才写出来，一朝吟出不禁泪流满面。)

It took me three years to get two lines right. / So when I chanted them, my tears flowed. (Jia Dao: After Finishing a Poem)

◎吟安一个字，捻断数茎须。(卢延让《苦吟》)
(琢磨出一个恰当的字，捻断了好几根胡须。)

Chanting in search of the right word, / I twisted off several hairs of my beard. (Lu Yanrang: Painstaking Versification)

kuāshì 夸饰

Exaggeration and Embellishment

文学作品中所使用的夸张和藻饰的创作手法。目的是增加艺术感染力，吸引读者注意，夸饰运用得好，可以达到写实无法企及的艺术效果，但是过度运用，则会产生华而不实的反面作用，因而古人提出了"夸而有节"的观点，主张夸饰要善于把握尺度。

The term refers to the use of exaggeration and embellishment in a literary work to enhance its artistic appeal. When used as appropriate, exaggeration and embellishment can achieve an artistic effect beyond that of realistic descriptions. However, if overused, it will create the opposite effect, making the writing too flowery to be credible. Therefore, the literary critics of old China believed that excessive use of exaggeration and embellishment should be avoided.

引例 Citations：

◎故自天地以降，豫入声貌，文辞所被，夸饰恒存。(刘勰《文心雕龙·夸饰》)

（因此，自从天地万物生成，就先有了各种声音和形貌，只要用文辞进行描述，夸张和藻饰的手法就会一直存在。）

Therefore, ever since the beginning of heaven and earth, there have been sounds and outward forms. So long as words are used to describe them, exaggeration and embellishment will always be employed. (Liu Xie: *The Literary Mind and the Carving of Dragons*)

◎使夸而有节，饰而不诬，亦可谓之懿也。（刘勰《文心雕龙·夸饰》）

（使得夸张而有节制，藻饰而不虚假，也就可以称为佳作了。）

When exaggeration is used in a restrained way and embellishment is employed without pretensions, a literary work thus created can be considered an excellent one. (Liu Xie: *The Literary Mind and the Carving of Dragons*)

lètiān-zhīmìng 乐天知命

Rejoice in Complying with Heaven and Know Its Mandate

乐于顺从天道并知晓命运的分限。出自《周易·系辞上》。天道规定了人事的法则，命运界定了人力的限度。这些都是人不能改易的，人应该知晓并坦然面对。同时，人在天、命的规范与限度内，又可以通过自身的不断努力，修养德行，拓展功业，故乐于顺从天、命。

Rejoice in complying with the way of heaven and recognize the limitations set by the mandate of heaven. This concept originates from *The Book of Changes*. The way of heaven regulates human affairs and its mandate defines the limit of human power. This is beyond human capacity to change, which man must understand and face with calm. While people are subject to regulation and limitation by Heaven and its mandate, they can cultivate their virtue and make great achievements through continuous efforts. That's why people should rejoice in complying with Heaven and its mandate.

引例 Citation：

◎旁行而不流，乐天知命，故不忧。（《周易·系辞上》）

（[圣人]能应变旁通而不会毫无节制，乐于顺从天道并知晓命运的分限，因此不会有忧虑。)

[A sage] can adapt appropriately to the changes of things without going too far. They rejoice in complying with the way of heaven and recognize the limitations set by the mandate of heaven, and so are free from anxiety. (*The Book of Changes*)

lí jiānbái 离坚白

Separate Hardness from Whiteness

分离一个事物所具有的坚和白的属性。"离坚白"是公孙龙子（前320？—前250）提出的一个命题。一块坚硬的白石，当眼睛看它时，只能看到石之白，看不到石之坚；当手触摸它时，只能摸到石之坚，摸不到石之白。坚与白是相互分离的，不能同时出现在石头上，因此不能将坚硬的白石称为"坚白石"。公孙龙子借由"坚白石"的例子，表达了对于事物属性的认识。事物的各种属性是相互独立的，不能同时关联在同一个事物中。

The separation of an object's hardness from its whiteness is a proposition advanced by Gongsunlongzi (320?-250 BC). Looking at a hard and white stone, one can only see its whiteness but not its hardness; while touching the stone with one's hand, one can only feel its hardness but not that it is white. Hardness and whiteness are separate. They do not manifest themselves at the same time: thus, a white stone that is hard cannot be called a hard and white stone. Gongsunlongzi used this example to express his understanding of the properties of things. These properties are independent of each other and cannot simultaneously be joined in the same thing.

引例 Citation：

◎视不得其所坚，而得其所白者，无坚也；拊不得其所白，而得其所坚者，无白也。(《公孙龙子·坚白论》)

（眼睛看不到石之坚，只能看到石之白，因此石是"无坚"的；手触摸不到石之白，只能触摸到石之坚，因此石是"无白"的。）

Looking at it, one cannot see the hardness of the stone but only the whiteness, so it has no hardness. Touching it, one cannot feel the whiteness but only the hardness, so it has no whiteness. (*Gongsunlongzi*)

líxíng-désì 离形得似

Transcend the Outer Form to Capture the Essence

　　文艺创作描绘对象时要善于超越外形而捕捉其精神特征，达到高度真实。庄子（前369？—前286）认为生命的根本在于精神而非形体，应该忘记形体存在而让精神自由驰骋。晚唐诗人司空图（837—908）借鉴这一观点，认为诗歌描绘对象也要追求神似而超越形似。这一诗歌创作理念和批评术语后来也在书法、绘画领域得到贯彻。

When describing something, literary writing should be able to go beyond external appearance to capture the essence so as to reflect a high degree of reality. Zhuangzi (369?-286 BC) considered that the essence of life lies in the inner spirit rather than the physical form. One should forget one's physical existence and give full free rein to the spirit. The late Tang poet Sikong Tu (837-908) adopted this view and believed that poetic description should likewise focus on essence rather than form. This concept of poetic creation and critique was later applied in calligraphy and painting as well.

引例 Citations：

◎有生必先无离形，形不离而生亡者有之矣。(《庄子·达生》)
(生命的存在必定要以形体健全为前提，但是形体没有离开生命而生命已经死亡的人也是有的啊。)

Life exists in a physical body. However, there are people who are dead due to lack of spirit although they are alive physically. (*Zhuangzi*)

◎离形得似，庶几斯人。(司空图《二十四诗品·形容》)
(做到离形得似，那才是真正善于描写对象的诗人。)

He who can transcend the outer form aside and capture the essence is truly a great poet. (Sikong Tu: Twenty-four Styles of Poetry)

◎离形得似，书家上乘，然此中消息甚微，不可死在句下。(姚孟起《字学臆参》)
(做到离形得似，即是书法作品中的上乘之作，不过这其中的道理很微妙，不能死抠字面意思。)

The work that transcends the outer form and captures the essence is a masterpiece. However, the theory underpinning this ability is very subtle and is not to be understood mechanically. (Yao Mengqi: *Personal Reflections on the Art of Calligraphy*)

lící 丽辞

Ornate Parallel Style

骈文中运用两两相对的方式遣词造句。"丽"即骈俪、对偶。单音独体汉字比较容易形成前后两句对偶的结构，对偶句具有音节配合、意义呼应的整齐美、和谐美。古人借此术语肯定了语言的形式美但又坚持形式与内容相和谐，以最终创作出文质相符、尽善尽美的作品。

The term refers to a classical Chinese literary style generally known as "parallel prose," largely composed of couplets of phrases with similar structure. Monosyllabic Chinese words, each represented with a single written character, are fairly easy to arrange in pairs of expressions with semantic symmetry and prosodic harmony. The ornate parallel style highlights the beauty of the form of the language without neglecting the harmony between form and content; and it is employed to produce fine works of utmost beauty, with form and content reinforcing each other.

引例 Citations：

◎故丽辞之体，凡有四对：言对为易，事对为难，反对为优，正对为劣。（刘勰《文心雕龙·丽辞》）
（丽辞的格式，大凡有四种：文辞的对偶容易，事典的对偶困难，事理不同而旨趣相合的对偶最佳，物类不同而意义相同的对偶最差。）

Thus, the ornate parallel style has four types of couplets: matching words, which is easy; matching facts, which is difficult; matching contrast, which is excellent; and matching sameness, which is poor. (Liu Xie: *The Literary Mind and the*

Carving of Dragons)

◎若气无奇类，文乏异采，碌碌丽辞，则昏睡耳目。（刘勰《文心雕龙·丽辞》）

（如果文章在气势上并无奇异的地方，文辞上也缺乏特别精彩之处，有的只是很平常的对偶句，那就让人昏昏欲睡了。）

If a piece of writing has no original appeal, lacks imaginative polish and is full of crude and common parallel phrases, it will bore people to sleep. (Liu Xie: *The Literary Mind and the Carving of Dragons*)

línyuān-lǚbó 临渊履薄

Be Discreet as if Standing on Cliff Edge or Treading on Thin Ice

像濒临深渊或脚踩薄冰之时一样小心谨慎。"临渊""履薄"都是极为危险的处境，人在这样境遇中，应以专注而谨慎的态度行事，以避免危险。而对道德、礼法的坚守或对应所担当的职责，同样需要始终保持专注而谨慎的态度，任何的放松懈怠都可能造成不良的后果，因此要像"临渊履薄"一样，心存敬畏，谨言慎行。

Be discreet and watchful as if one is standing on the edge of a cliff or treading on thin ice, both being precarious situations in which people need to exercise maximum caution to stay safe. One should observe the same discreet and care when it comes to adherence to ethics, rites and law as well as fulfilling one's due responsibility. Any slackening may result in disastrous consequences. Hence the importance of being discreet and watchful.

引例 Citations：

◎不敢暴虎，不敢冯（píng）河。人知其一，莫知其他。战战兢兢，如临深渊，如履薄冰。(《诗经·小雅·小旻》)
(不敢徒手搏虎，不敢徒步渡河。人知道这些显见的祸患，不知其他的危险。应战战兢兢，如同濒临深渊，如同脚踩薄冰。)

People all know that they should not fight a tiger with bare hands or wade through a river, but they are not aware of other dangers. We should be discreet and watchful in dangerous situations as if to stand on the edge of a cliff or tread on thin ice. (*The Book of Songs*)

◎曾子有疾，召门弟子曰："启予足！启予手！《诗》云：'战战兢兢，如临深渊，如履薄冰。'而今而后，吾知免夫（fú）！小子！"(《论语·泰伯》)
(曾子患了疾病，召集他的学生说道："看看我的脚！看看我的手！《诗经》上说：'战战兢兢，如同濒临深渊，如同脚踩薄冰。'从今以后，我才知道自己是可以免于祸害刑戮的了！学生们！")

When Zengzi was ill, he summoned his students and said: "Look at my trembling feet and hands! *The Book of Songs* says, 'One should be fearful, discreet and watchful, as if standing on the edge of a cliff or treading on thin ice.' I am now in such a state and I know I may stay away from disasters and punishments, my students!" (*The Analects*)

liùguān 六观

Six Criteria

文章鉴赏和批评的六个角度，亦是文章本身所具有的六方面要素，包括

"位体"（谋篇布局）、"置辞"（遣词造句）、"通变"（对前人作品风格的继承与创新）、"奇正"（表现手法上的守正与新变）、"事义"（援引事例以证立论）、"宫商"（音律节奏）。"六观"作为批评方法论，是《文心雕龙》整个理论体系的重要一环，它使文章批评自此有章可循，避免了批评的主观性，对后世的诗文评论有着指导与规范的作用，也对现代文学理论建构具有显著影响。

The term refers to the following six criteria on literary appreciation and criticism which are also six key elements in writing: structural layout of writing, choice of words to construct sentences, acceptance and innovation in the style of earlier writers, inheriting and transforming traditional ways of expression, citing examples to support an argument, and musical rhythm. As a school of literary criticism, the six criteria formed a key component in the theoretical system established in *The Literary Mind and the Carving of Dragons*. The six criteria offered rules that could be followed to avoid subjectivity in literary criticism. They also provided a framework of theoretical guidance for later generations of critics and exerted significant influence on the development of literary theory in modern times.

引例 Citation：

◎是以将阅文情，先标六观：一观位体，二观置辞，三观通变，四观奇正，五观事义，六观宫商。（刘勰《文心雕龙·知音》）
（因此阅读和评论文章，先要标明需要考察的六个方面：一是谋篇布局，二是遣词造句，三是对前人作品风格的继承与创新，四是表现手法上的守正与新变，五是援引事例以证立论，六是音律节奏。）

Therefore, we should study and comment a literary work according to the following six criteria: structural layout of writing, choice of words to construct sentences, acceptance and innovation in the style of earlier writers, inheriting and transforming traditional ways of expression, citing examples to support an argument, and musical rhythm. (Liu Xie: *The Literary Mind and the Carving of Dragons*)

liùyì 六艺

The Six Arts

"六艺"有两种不同的含义：其一，指《诗》《书》《礼》《乐》《易》《春秋》六部经典。历代儒者通过对"六经"文本的不断解释，为这些经典赋予了丰富的意义。"六艺"之学体现着古人对于世界秩序与价值的根本理解。其二，指礼、乐、射、御、书、数六种技能，是古代学校教育的基本内容。

The six arts may refer to two sets of content. They may refer to the Six Classics: *The Book of Songs*, *The Book of History*, *The Book of Rites*, *The Book of Music*, *The Book of Changes*, and *The Spring and Autumn Annals*. Confucian scholars through the ages kept interpreting these classical texts, endowing them with rich significance. Theories related to the six arts represent the basic views of the ancients in regard to world order and values. The six arts may also refer to the six skills of rituals, music, archery, charioteering, writing, and mathematics, which were the basic contents of school teaching in antiquity.

引例 Citations：

◎六艺者，王教之典籍，先圣所以明天道、正人伦、致至治之成法也。(《汉书·儒林传序》)

("六艺"是王道教化所使用的典籍,是古代圣人用来彰明天道、端正人伦、实现治世的既成的法则。)

The six arts are the canons of kingly instruction by which the ancient sages expounded the way of heaven, set human relationships right, and kept the society in peace and order. (*The History of the Han Dynasty*)

◎保氏:掌谏王恶,而养国子以道。乃教之六艺:一曰五礼,二曰六乐,三曰五射,四曰五驭,五曰六书,六曰九数。(《周礼·地官·保氏》)

(保氏的职责:负责匡正君王的恶行,而以正道教导国中王公贵胄的子弟。于是教给他们"六艺":其一是五个方面的礼仪,其二是六种乐舞,其三是五种射箭之法,其四是五种驾车之法,其五是汉字的六种造字方法,其六是九种计数之法。)

Responsibilities of the Palace Education Guardian: admonishing the king against wrongdoing and tutoring the scions of state in the right principles. Thus he teaches them the six arts: the five types of ritual, the six styles of music and dance, the five ways of archery, the five methods of charioteering, the six ways of creating written characters, and the nine types of mathematics. (*The Rites of Zhou*)

máodùn 矛盾

Paradox of the Spear and the Shield / Contradiction

可以刺穿任何东西的矛和没有任何东西能够刺穿的盾。"矛盾"之说出自《韩非子》。可以刺穿任何东西的矛和没有任何东西能够刺穿的盾,这两个命题是不相容的。一个人不能同时肯定这样两个不相容的命题。后世即以

"矛盾"指称事物之间的对立关系，也意指言行自相抵触。

The term comes from a story in *Hanfeizi*. In the story, *mao* (矛) is a spear that is said to be able to pierce anything; *dun* (盾) is a shield that is said to be able to be pierced by nothing. *Mao* and *dun* are a paradox to each other, so a person cannot affirm both propositions at the same time. Later, the term came to mean "contradiction," or "inconsistency between speech and action."

引例 Citation：

◎ 楚人有鬻楯（dùn）与矛者，誉之曰："吾楯之坚，物莫能陷也。"又誉其矛曰："吾矛之利，于物无不陷也。"或曰："以子之矛，陷子之楯，何如？"其人弗能应也。夫不可陷之楯与无不陷之矛，不可同世而立。(《韩非子·难（nàn）一》)

(有一位楚国人，既卖矛又卖盾，他夸赞自己的盾说："我的盾坚硬无比，没有任何东西能刺穿它。"又夸赞自己的矛说："我的矛非常锋利，任何东西都可以刺穿。"有人问他："那如果用你的矛刺你的盾，结果会怎么样呢？"楚国人无法回答。任何东西都无法刺穿的盾和能够刺穿一切的矛，不可能同时存在于这个世界中。)

A man from the State of Chu was selling spears and shields. He boasted about his shield, saying "It is so tough that nothing can pierce it." He then boasted about his spear, saying, "It is so sharp that it can pierce anything." Someone asked him, "What will happen if you pierce your shield using your spear?" The man was speechless. A spear that can pierce anything and a shield that can be pierced by nothing cannot exist at the same time. (*Hanfeizi*)

mǐ bù yǒu chū, xiǎn kè yǒu zhōng 靡不有初，鲜克有终

All Things Have a Beginning, but Few Can Reach the End.

所有的事情都会有开始，但很少有人能够做到善终。"靡"，无，没有；"初"，开始；"鲜"，很少；"克"，能够。语出《诗经·大雅·荡》。原本斥责周厉王昏庸无道，政令多变而为害百姓。"靡不有初，鲜克有终"具有深刻的现实意义和哲学意义，做人、做事、为官、理政，有一个好的开端并不难，难的是始终如一地坚持到最后。它告诫我们，做事情不要轻易更改，不能开始时信誓旦旦但很快就忘记初衷，更不能轻言放弃，一定要做到有始有终、善始善终。

All undertakings have a beginning, but few people are able to see things through to the end. *Mi* (靡) means "nothing, none," and *chu* (初) means "beginning." *Xian* (鲜) means "few," and *ke* (克) means "be able, can." The saying comes from *The Book of Songs*, and was a criticism of the degenerate and immoral King Li of Zhou whose constantly changing decrees brought misery to his people. The story has both practical and philosophical implications. Starting off with a flourish is not difficult, whether in personal behavior, doing business, being an official or governing a country. It's persevering to the end that is hardest. This is an admonition to us to not keep changing our minds, to avoid making bold early promises and then failing to live up to them. We must not give up in the middle, but should persevere so that things not only begin well but also end well.

引例 Citation：

◎天生烝民，其命匪谌（chén）。靡不有初，鲜克有终。(《诗经·大雅·荡》)

(上天生下众百姓，政令不能无诚信。凡事都会有开始，很少有人能善终。)

Heaven created all people. Decrees of government must be consistent. All things have a beginning, but few people can see them through to the end. (*The Book of Songs*)

miàosuàn 庙算

Court Calculation

朝廷对军国大事的谋算。"庙"为庙堂，是古代朝廷议事之所。"庙算"即是于战争开始之前，在庙堂之上郑重地谋算战争中己方的优势、劣势，从而决定应对策略。孙武认为，战争不只是战场上的争斗，还受到政治、经济等不同因素的影响。因此"庙算"需要结合可能的战争态势，对国家各方面的情况进行综合评判与谋算。"庙算"是战争准备的必要环节。

This term means court calculation on major military and state affairs. The imperial court here refers to the place for officials to deliberate on affairs of state in ancient China. The purpose of calculation prior to war was to work out a strategy based on the state's strengths and weaknesses. Sunzi's view was that war was not merely a contest on the battlefield, but was also influenced by political, economic and other factors. Court calculation thus had to take into account different war scenarios and review a full range of circumstances in the state. Court calculation was a necessary preparation for war.

引例 Citation：

◎夫未战而庙算胜者，得算多也；未战而庙算不胜者，得算少也。多算胜，

少算不胜，而况于无算乎！吾以此观之，胜负见矣。(《孙子·始计》)
（开战之前做军事谋划而获胜的，是因为谋划周详；开战之前做军事谋划而失败的，是因为谋划不够周详。谋划周详则获胜，谋划不周详则失利，何况是全无谋划的呢！我以这样的方法去观察，战争的胜败就可以预见了。）

Those who make court calculation before battle and win must have been thorough in the process. Those who make calculation before battle and lose must have been insufficient in the process. Thorough calculation leads to victory, insufficient calculation leads to defeat – to say nothing of no calculation at all! When I look at warfare in this way, victory and defeat become obvious. (*The Art of War*)

míngdé 明德

Illustrious Virtue

有两种含义：其一，彰显美德；其二，指光明或纯明的德性。"明德"最初是对为政者的一种要求。"德"特指为政者在照顾百姓、任用官吏、施加赏罚等方面的良好品行。"明德"即是在施政中遵循并彰显这些德行。后世用"明德"指称为政者应该具备的显明的品德。而在儒家看来，为政之德是人的内在德性的扩充，因此为政者的"明德"即体现着至高的道德。

This term has two meanings. First, it means to manifest rectitude. Second, it refers to upright conduct. The term was originally used to describe qualities expected of the sovereign. *De* (德) specifically meant fairness and decency towards the populace, in the appointment of officials, and the bestowing of rewards and punishments. *Mingde* (明德) as a verb was to govern in such a way. Later, the term as a noun referred to the required moral qualities of those in power. Confucianism holds that governing in a moral way is an extension of a person's internal rectitude, hence *mingde* is an expression of the highest degree of morality manifested by a ruler.

引例 Citations：

◎惟乃丕显考文王，克明德慎罚，不敢侮鳏寡，庸庸，祗（zhī）祗，威威，显民。(《尚书·康诰》)

(你显赫的父亲周文王，能彰显美德，慎用刑罚，不敢侮慢鳏寡之人，任用可用之人，敬重可敬之人，威慑需要被威慑之人，向民众显示这些美德。)

Your illustrious father King Wen of Zhou displayed virtue to his people. He punished sparingly, did not disrespect the bereaved, appointed those with ability, recognized those with good qualities, and intimidated those who needed to be deterred. (*The Book of History*)

◎大学之道，在明明德，在亲民，在止于至善。(《礼记·大学》)

(大学的宗旨，在于彰显光明的德性，在于亲和民众，在于达到言行的至善。)

Great Learning aims to foster moral integrity, forge close ties with the people and attain consummate virtue in both words and deeds. (*The Book of Rites*)

míngfèn-shǐqún 明分使群

Proper Ranking Leads to Collaboration.

明确个人的职分差等以组成能够相互协作的群体。荀子（前313？—

前238）将"能群"看作是人区别于禽兽的重要特征。而人在没有约束的情况下，会出于自身对外物的欲求，与人争夺，进而导致群体的混乱。因此，在群体之中必须依据道义的原则，明确个人分位的差等以及与之相应的职责、权益，并以此作为人与人相处的规范，从而约束彼此间的纷争，实现相互协作。

Group collaboration is possible only when the individuals within it are clearly ranked and there is a social order. For Xunzi (313?-238 BC), the ability to "work together" is what distinguishes humans from animals. Without social restraints, humans will follow their innate desires and fight over things, causing disruption within the group. That is why there must be appropriate rules for people of different ranks, with clear rights and responsibilities to guide proper conduct, which will limit discord and build collaboration.

引例 Citations：

◎［人］力不若牛，走不若马，而牛马为用，何也？曰：人能群，彼不能群也。人何以能群？曰：分（fēn）。分何以能行？曰：义。故义以分则和，和则一，一则多力，多力则强，强则胜物。(《荀子·王制》)

（人的力量不如牛，奔跑的能力不如马，但牛马却被人驱使，是什么原因呢？回答道：因为人能够组成分工协作的群体，那些牛马不能。人依据什么能够组成分工协作的群体？回答道：依靠名分差等。名分差等依据什么能够施行？回答道：依据道义。因此依据道义来区分差等则能够彼此和谐，和谐则能统一，统一则能凝聚力量，凝聚力量则强大，强大则胜过万物。）

Man is not as strong as the ox, and cannot run as fast as the horse. Yet man is able to use them both. How is this possible? Answer: humans can work together, while animals cannot. How is it people can work together? Answer: by having different ranks and positions. How do the ranks and positions operate? Answer: by applying correct rules of conduct. By applying these rules there can be harmony, with harmony there is unity, with unity there is strength, with strength everything can be overcome. (*Xunzi*)

◎离居不相待则穷,群而无分(fèn)则争。穷者患也,争者祸也,救患除祸,则莫若明分使群矣。(《荀子·富国》)

(离开群体独处而不相互依靠,则会穷困;居处在一起而没有分位差等,则会相互争夺。穷苦和争夺都是祸患,而要解救、免除祸患,没有什么比得上明分使群。)

Living alone without group support leads to poverty; living together without appropriate ranking causes disputes. Poverty and disputes are all disastrous. The best way to solve these problems is to establish different ranks, which makes collaboration possible. (*Xunzi*)

mùjī-dàocún 目击道存

See the Way with One's Own Eyes

视野所及而瞬时感悟到"道"的存在。源自《庄子》。庄子(前369?—前286)强调人可以直观感悟到"道"的存在,而无需依赖语言说明和逻辑思辨。后被用于文学创作与鉴赏领域,强调超越耳目感知和逻辑思辨,在涤除一切杂念和外物干扰的心境中领悟并臻于最高的艺术境界。这一术语意在彰显文艺审美中直观感悟与超越功利的特性。

The term, which first appeared in the Chinese classic writing *Zhuangzi* (Zhuangzi 369?-286 BC), means that one can easily see the existence of Dao with no need to rely on verbal explanation or on logical analysis. Later it was used for literary creations and in the field of connoisseurship. The concept emphasizes the need for one to transcend audio and visual perceptions and logical analysis, and do away with any interfering thoughts or external objects in order to attain true appreciation of art. The concept highlights the importance of seeking intuitive insights unaffected by utilitarian considerations in literature and art.

引例 Citations：

◎子路曰："吾子欲见温伯雪子久矣。见之而不言，何邪？"仲尼曰："若夫人者，目击而道存矣，亦不可以容声矣！"(《庄子·田子方》)

(子路说："先生您想见温伯雪子很久了。见了他却又不说话，为什么呢？"孔子说："像他这种人，只要一见就明白他身上存有的道，无需再用声音表达了。")

Zilu said: "You, Master, have been wanting to see Wenbo Xuezi for a long time. But you did not say a word when you saw him. Why?" Confucius replied: "As soon as I saw him, I realized that he possesses the Dao! So there was no need for me to say anything." (*Zhuangzi*)

◎夫置意作诗，即须凝心，目击其物，便以心击之，深穿其境。如登高山绝顶，下临万象，如在掌中。(王昌龄《诗格·论文意》)

(当有作诗的打算，就应该凝聚心神，眼睛盯着想要吟咏的物体，用心去接触体会，深深穿透眼前之物而臻于诗的情境。就像登上高山绝顶，向下俯视万物，一切都好像掌握在自己手中。)

If you intend to compose a poem, you should concentrate your mind on it. Fix your eyes on the object which you want to admire in your poem, and appreciate it with your heart. By doing so, you will reach a perfect realm of poetic reflection, as if you have reached the summit of a high mountain, obtained a panoramic view of everything below and gained full command of them. (Wang Changling: *Rules of Poetry*)

nánxì 南戏

Southern Opera

指北宋末年至明末清初流行于南方的汉族戏文。其源头是宋室南渡之时，产生于温州地区的戏种，在当时被称作传奇、戏文等，又被称为温州杂剧、永嘉杂剧、永嘉戏曲等。其特点是将民间唱腔引入杂剧，在村坊小曲的基础上发展起来，起初没有宫调、节奏方面的讲究，只是顺口可歌而已。元代高明（1301？—1370？）创作的《琵琶记》，标志着南戏体制的完备。南戏继承了宋代杂剧，开启明代传奇，篇幅长，角色丰富，而且各种角色都可演唱。《荆钗记》《刘知远白兔记》《拜月亭》《杀狗记》是南戏代表作。我国南方戏曲中有多种声腔都是在南戏基础上发展起来的。

Nanxi (南戏), the Southern Opera, refers to the Han ethnic opera from the late Northern Song to the late Ming and the early Qing dynasties. The opera was created in the Wenzhou region when the Song court fled south. At the time, it was also known as *chuanqi* (传奇 legendary play), *xiwen* (戏文 opera) as well as the Wenzhou *Zaju* (温州杂剧 Wenzhou Opera), the Yongjia *Zaju* (永嘉杂剧 Yongjia Opera), and the Yongjia *Xiqu* (永嘉戏曲 Yongjia Play). Drawing on local folk singing styles, the Southern Opera first developed on the basis of village operas without any traces of musical modes and rhymes, and it was noted for being natural and smooth in singing. *A Tale of the Pipa*, a play by Gao Ming (1301?-1370?), marked the maturity of the Southern Opera. The Southern Opera inherited the Song *zaju* and heralded the emergence of the legendary play of the Ming Dynasty. Legendary plays were long enough to accommodate multiple roles and all performers sang. The Southern Opera masterpieces include *The Romance of a Hairpin*, *The Story of the White Rabbit*, *The Moonlight Pavilion*, and *The Killing of a Dog*. Many operas in southern China were created based on the Southern Opera.

引例 Citations：

◎龙楼景、丹墀秀皆金门高之女也，俱有姿色，专工南戏。（夏庭芝《青楼集》）

（龙楼景、丹墀秀都是金门高的女儿，都长得很漂亮，擅长表演南戏。）

Longloujing and Danchixiu were both daughters of Jinmengao. They were beautiful and good at giving South Opera performances. (Xia Tingzhi: *Biographies of Courtesans*)

◎金元人呼北戏为杂剧，南戏为戏文。（何良俊《四友斋丛说·词曲》）

（金、元时代的人把北戏称作杂剧，南戏称作戏文。）

The Northern Opera was known as *zaju* and the Southern Opera as *xiwen* in the Jin and Yuan dynasties. (He Liangjun: *Academic Notes from the Four-scholar Study*)

nǐróng-qǔxīn 拟容取心

Compare Appearances to Grasp the Essence

指诗人在采取比兴手法的时候，通过类比、描摹事物的形象外貌，摄取事物内在的意蕴和义理，从而将原本不同的事物联系、结合在一起。"拟容"说的是重视"比兴"的具体形象；"取心"说的是摄取事物的精神实质，即重视事物形象所包含的内在意蕴和理趣。合起来的意思是，借助能表达一定意义的事物形象，来寄寓、抒写作者的思想感情。见于《文心雕龙·比兴》，由《周易·系辞上》中的"拟物立象"发展而来。刘勰（465？—520）提出这一术语，主要用以阐释比、兴都是由彼及此，二者又有不同：比为"拟容"，重在贴合事理，忌不伦不类；兴为"取心"，重在感发幽微，以意相联。

This term means a poet uses the techniques of analogy and stimulation to depict the form and the external appearance of things. He takes in internal connotations and the principles of things, thus linking originally different things and combining them. *Nirong* (拟容 comparing appearances) attaches importance to specific forms for *bixing* (比兴 analogy and stimulation). While *quxin* (取心 grasping the essence) aims to get at the spirit and the essence of things, it therefore attaches importance to internal connotations and to the principles contained in the form of things. The combined meaning is that by giving expression to the form of things with a certain meaning, one may imply and express his thoughts and feelings. This notion appeared in *The Literary Mind and the Carving of Dragons*. It developed from *niwu lixiang* (拟物立象 create images through object imitation) in *The Book of Changes*. Liu Xie (465?-520) first used this term, mainly to explain that analogy and stimulation are interconnected but are different: Analogy here means "comparing appearances."

Staying true to the principle of things is most important, and anything far-fetched should be avoided. Stimulation means "grasping the essence," sensing the abstruse and being connected with the meaning.

引例 Citations：

◎诗人比兴，触物圆览。物虽胡越，合则肝胆。拟容取心，断辞必敢。攒杂咏歌，如川之涣。（刘勰《文心雕龙·比兴》）

（诗人在运用比兴手法的时候，能够具体周密地接触、观察事物。即使事物的差异很大，像胡、越一样遥不相及，用比兴合在一起却如同肝胆那样密切。比拟、描摹事物的外在形象，摄取事物的内在意蕴和理趣，判断和措辞一定要果断明白。把繁杂纷纭的事物用比兴纳入诗歌，文思就如同河水一样畅快流淌。）

When a poet uses analogy and stimulation, he comes into close contact with things and observes them thoroughly. Things may be quite disorganized, but when combined they tend to show themselves to be intimately linked. When comparing appearances to grasp the essence of things, one should be concise and resolute in forming judgment. When one incorporates various things in recitations and songs, they will swell and flow like a river. (Liu Xie: *The Literary Mind and the Carving of Dragons*)

◎取象曰比，取义曰兴，义即象下之意。（释皎然《诗式·用事》）

（从事物的外部形象方面着眼是"比"，从事物的内在意蕴方面着眼是"兴"，而意蕴就含在形象之中。）

Analogy means comparing the appearances of things, while association means grasping the essence of things. Meaning is what underlies the appearance. (Shi Jiaoran: *Poetic Styles*)

nián 年

Lunar Year / Year

在文字学意义上，"年"的本义指庄稼成熟，即年成。因庄稼大都一岁一熟，"年"渐等同于"岁"，成为历法上的时间单位（一年），后又引申指年节（春节）。在历法意义上，它是指中国传统农历（阴阳合历）的一个时间周期，平年12个月，大月30天，小月29天，全年354或355天；闰年13个月，全年383、384或385天。作为一个时间周期，它与中国古代的农业生产密切相关，反映农耕社会的时间意识和思想观念。近代以来，西方的历法（公历）传入中国，1912年为中华民国正式采用，形成了公历与农历并行的双历法系统，所以"年"现在既指农历的时间周期，也指公历的时间周期，视具体的语境而定。

In the literal sense, the Chinese character *nian* (年) means the ripening of crops. As crops are mostly harvested annually, the Chinese character *nian* has gradually come to refer to the period of one year, and later it is used to refer to the annual Spring Festival. When it comes to the calendar, it refers to the period of one year on the lunar calendar (lunisolar calendar), which has 12 months: 7 months each of 30 days and 5 months of 29 days, altogether 354 or 355 days. A leap year has 13 months, altogether 383 or 384 or 385 days a year. As a lunar calendar, it is closely related to agricultural production cycles in ancient China, and it epitomizes ancient Chinese people's awareness of time and concept in an agrarian society. The Gregorian calendar from the West was adopted by the Republic of China in 1912, ushering in a dual system of lunar and solar calendars. As a result, *nian* (year) refers to a year on the solar or lunar calendar, depending on the context.

引例 Citation：

◎年年岁岁花相似，岁岁年年人不同。(刘希夷《代悲白头翁》)
(每年繁花盛开十分相似，但是前来赏花的人却不同。)

Blossoms look the same season after season; but people enjoying the flowers look different from year to year. (Liu Xiyi: Feeling Sorry for a White-haired Old Man)

pǐntí 品题

Make Appraisals

对人的品行、才干、风貌等进行品评，判断其高下。盛行于汉末魏晋时期。品题在初兴时具有一定的进步意义，看人不论出身，只论德行才华，是鉴别人才、量才授官的重要手段。魏晋人士清谈的内容之一就是对于人物的识鉴和品藻，当时称为"题目"。但自魏末晋初开始，对人物的品评逐渐倾向于门第权势，九品中正制的形成与此有关。另一方面，品题由对人物的品评转向对于诗文书画的品评，选拔人才的功用削弱，艺术审美的意义凸显，这种风尚影响到南北朝的文学批评，催生了各种诗品、画品、书品等批评著作的出现。

This concept means appraising someone's character, ability, conduct and approach, which was a common practice from the late Han through the Jin and Wei dynasties. The practice was considered a good one when it was first introduced, as people were judged by their moral character and ability, not their family background, making it an important means of selecting officials based on their competence. Appraisal of others was a popular conversational topic among the people in the Wei and Jin dynasties. However, such appraisal gradually shifted towards people's family status, power and influence in the late Wei and early Jin dynasties, which led to the establishment of the nine-rank system for selecting and appointing government officials. There was also a shift in making appraisals away from people towards poetry, paintings and calligraphic works. Thus making appraisals played a less important role in selecting officials while assuming a more significant role in the appreciation of art. This influenced literary criticism in the Southern and Northern Dynasties and led to the creation of works of literary critique on poetry, paintings and calligraphy.

引例 Citations：

◎［许］劭与［许］靖俱有高名，好共覈（hé）论乡党人物，每月辄更其品题，故汝南俗有"月旦评"焉。(《后汉书·许劭传》)

（许劭和许靖都有名望，喜欢聚在一起详细苛刻评论同乡的人物，每个月都要更换品评的对象，所以汝南的人称他们为"月旦（每月初一）评"。）

Xu Shao and Xu Jing were both celebrities in Runan who liked to comment on their fellow townsmen and changed the subjects they commented on every month. What they did was referred to by the locals as "making monthly appraisals." (*The History of the Later Han Dynasty*)

◎诸英志录，并义在文，曾（zēng）无品第。嵘今所录，止乎五言。虽然，网罗今古，词文殆集。轻欲辨彰清浊，掎摭（jǐzhí）病利，凡百二十人。(钟嵘《诗品》卷中)

（诸位名家编选的总集，意在收罗文章，并没有品评作品的高下。我的《诗品》收录，仅限于五言诗。然而古今的诗人以及他们的代表作品差不多搜罗殆尽了。我就是要辨明诗人的高下，指出作品的优劣，共计品评了一百二十人。）

Compilations of works of famous authors are meant to bring works together on an extensive basis rather than comparing their literary attainment. *The Critique of Poetry* I have compiled, however, is a selection of five-character regulated verses only. As almost all the poets and their masterpieces are already included in other compilations, mine just includes the works of 120 poets, with comments on the merits and demerits of their works. (Zhong Rong: *The Critique of Poetry*)

qízhèng 奇正

Qi or Zheng (Surprise or Normal)

"奇"是反常的、出其不意的，"正"是正面的、正常的。最早由《老子》提出。主要含义有二：其一，作为军事用语，指两种不同的用兵应敌的方式："正"指在了解敌方作战意图基础上的正面应敌，"奇"指隐蔽自己的作战意图，灵活地运用偷袭、设伏等手段，以达到出其不意的效果。"奇"与"正"的运用需要相互配合。"奇正"有时也被用来处理、应对日常事务。其二，作为文艺批评术语，用来称说文章思想内容上的纯正与奇诡以及文辞上的典雅与巧丽。南朝刘勰（465？—520）为了矫正齐梁时期的文坛过于重形式、片面追求新奇的弊病，将"奇正"引入文学批评。他认为，文学创作应当在思想内容上以儒家经典为依归，以文辞上的巧丽奇异为配合，只有执"正"（思想纯正）以驭"奇"（文辞巧丽），才能使文章的主旨新颖而不邪乱，词采美丽而不浮夸。后世诗歌评论及戏曲批评也用到这一术语。

Qi (奇) means surprise while *zheng* (正) means direct and normal. First advanced by Laozi, the concept has two main meanings. First, it is a military term about two opposing ways of fighting. *Zheng* means meeting the enemy head-on based on an understanding of its intention, while *Qi* means keeping one's intention to oneself and launching surprise attack and laying ambush on the enemy in order to secure surprise victory. *Zheng* and *qi* need to be applied in a coordinated way. While a military term, *qizheng* is also used to deal with daily affairs. Second, as a term of literary and art criticism, it means an article is pure and original in terms of theme and elegant and stylish in terms of diction. Liu Xie (465?–520) of the Southern Dynasty first introduced *qizheng* in literary criticism to oppose attaching excessive importance to form and novelty, a trend which was popular in the literary circles in the Qi and Liang dynasties. Liu Xie maintained that literary creation should be based on Confucian classics in terms of theme, to be embellished by stylish rhetoric. He believed that pure thought (*zheng*) must come before rhetoric (*qi*) so that an essay would be original in terms of theme and beautiful but unexaggerated in terms of diction. The term *qizheng* was later also used in literary criticism of poetry and opera.

引例 Citations：

◎ 以正治国，以奇用兵，以无事取天下。(《老子·五十七章》)
（以正规的方式（清静之道）治国，以奇诡的方法用兵，以不搅扰人民来治理天下。）

A state should be ruled by the normal way, fighting should be conducted in a surprised way, while ideal governance should let people handle their own affairs. (*Laozi*)

◎凡战者，以正合，以奇胜。故善出奇者，无穷如天地，不竭如江海。(《孙子·兵势》)

(大凡用兵作战，都是以正面应敌，以奇兵取胜。所以善于出奇的人，出奇用兵的手段像大地那样无穷无尽，像江海那样长流不竭。)

In all warfare, the direct way is to meet enemy attack head-on, but surprise attack should be launched in order to secure victory. One who is good at using surprise attack will have at his disposal a rich reservoir of such tactics as inexhaustible as Heaven and Earth and as unending as the flow of rivers and streams. (*The Art of War*)

◎是以将阅文情，先标六观：一观位体，二观置辞，三观通变，四观奇正，五观事义，六观宫商。(刘勰《文心雕龙·知音》)

(因此阅读和评论文章，先要标明需要考察的六个方面：一是谋篇布局，二是遣词造句，三是对前人作品风格的继承与创新，四是表现手法上的守正与新变，五是援引事例以证立论，六是音律节奏。)

Therefore, we should study and comment a literary work according to the following six criteria: structural layout of writing, choice of words to construct sentences, acceptance and innovation in the style of earlier writers, inheriting and transforming traditional ways of expression, citing examples to support an argument, and musical rhythm. (Liu Xie: *The Literary Mind and the Carving of Dragons*)

qiyùn 气韵

Artistic Appeal

指绘画、书法、文学中所流露出的气势、韵致和生机，是文学艺术作品整体给人的审美感觉。最初仅用于绘画，指用墨、用笔恰当，作品就能表现出自然山水的意态，画幅上就会有流动的生机，令人体味到笔墨之外的精神、韵味。后来逐渐由绘画扩大到诗文、书法等领域。在实际应用中，与"风韵""神韵"等术语近似，是需要借助经验、感悟来获得的审美感觉。气韵虽然通过作品呈现，却与艺术家本人的格调、心胸直接相关，属于自然天成，不能刻意获得。

This refers to the momentum, charm, and vitality in paintings as well as in calligraphic and literary works which together create artistic appeals. The term was first used to refer only to painting, meaning that the proper use of ink and the painting brush could vividly present natural landscape, make the painting flow with vitality, and enable viewers to appreciate its underlying allure. Later, the term was extended to cover poetry, essay, calligraphy and other literary creations. Artistic appeal, which is similar in meaning to such terms as artistic charm and literary charm, is an aesthetic appreciation gained through experiences and feelings. Expressed in a work of art, artistic appeal reflects an author's unique approach to art and inspiration, something that he is born with rather than acquired.

引例 Citations：

◎六法者何？一气韵生动是也，二骨法用笔是也，三应物象形是也，四随类

赋彩是也，五经营位置是也，六传移模写是也。（谢赫《古画品录》）
（绘画的六个法则是什么呢？其一是作品要充满生气，富有神韵；其二是运笔能自如呈现各种线条变化；其三是造型要顺应对象外形特征；其四是要根据对象特征进行着色；其五是构图要合理搭配，呈现整体效果；其六是要临摹佳作以传承前人画技。）

There are six rules for painting. A painting should be full of vitality and artistic appeal; the painting brush should be used in such a way as to make changes in lines natural; image painted should suit the appearance of the painted object; coloring should suit the features of the object portrayed; the painting should be well structured to present an overall visual effect; and masterpieces of past painters should be copied to draw inspiration from them. (Xie He: *An Appraisal of Ancient Paintings*)

◎气韵有笔墨间两种。墨中气韵，人多会得；笔端气韵，世每鲜（xiǎn）知。（方薰《山静居画论》卷上）
（气韵有两种，分别在笔之间、墨之间。用墨当中的气韵，人们多能领悟；笔端的气韵，世上很少有人知道。）

There are two types of artistic appeal in the use of ink and of the painting brush respectively. The artistic appeal created through the use of ink is readily appreciated; however, such appeal created through the use of the painting brush is not easy to appreciate. (Fang Xun: *On Painting in the Quiet Mountain Studio*)

qiānlǐzhīxíng, shǐyúzúxià 千里之行，始于足下

A Journey of a Thousand *Li* Begins with the First Step.

千里远的行程，要从迈第一步开始。比喻远大目标的实现，要从小的、基础的事情做起。足下：脚所站立的地方。语出《老子》。《老子》以大树、高台、千里之行一方面说明在问题或祸乱发生之前一定要提前防范或处置妥当，以免量变引起质变；另一方面说明任何事情都需要从头做起，一个好的开始往往是事情成败的关键，远大的理想和抱负需要脚踏实地地推进，才能在一个个具体目标的实现中完成看似不可能完成的任务。

Any major undertaking must start small from the basics. The expression comes from *Laozi*. *Zuxia* (足下) means the place where one is standing. Laozi used the metaphors of a giant tree, a high platform, a long journey to represent two different ideas. (1) Proper preventive measures must be taken before problems or troubles occur lest things become worse; (2) All undertakings must start from the very beginning, because success or failure often depends on a good start; an extension of this is that reaching distant ideals and aspirations depends on many practical steps along the way to attain the seemingly impossible goal.

引例 Citation：

◎合抱之木，生于毫末；九层之台，起于累土；千里之行，始于足下。(《老子·六十四章》)

（合抱的大树，是从细小的萌芽生长起来的；九层的高台，是一筐筐土筑起来的；千里远的行程，是从迈第一步开始的。）

The giant tree that needs several people to encircle grew from a tiny sapling; the platform nine stories high was built from piling many baskets of earth; and the journey of a thousand *li* begins with the first step. (*Laozi*)

qiānxiǎng-miàodé 迁想妙得

Inspirational Creation Based on Association in Thinking

指画家在艺术构思与创作过程中善于联想,将各种形象、素材通过画家的情感活动重新组织、构图,使画面形神兼备,如同妙手偶得。"迁想"重在想象、选择与构思,所创作的题材、素材来源于现实,却不是现实的完全复制。"迁想"是将画家的思想情感融进、移入作品的形象。"妙得"意思是精妙之得,是"迁想"的最终结果,重在作品的审美效果。它不仅要"得"物之形,还要"得"物之神,如此才称得上"妙",因此,"妙得"也有妙得灵感的意思。"迁想""妙得"是一个连贯的艺术创作过程,不可分割。这一术语是对艺术构思与审美活动特点的最早概括,后成为中国绘画理论中的一个重要原则。

This concept means a painter should be good at association in thinking in artistic conception and creation. He should give full rein to his imagination and connect and reconstruct a variety of source images and materials so as to create a great painting in both image and spirit. "Association in thinking" stresses imagination, selection, connection and conception. While the subject matter and source materials come from reality, the painting is by no means a replica of it. "Association in thinking" makes it possible for a painter to reconstruct his thoughts and emotions in the image of his work. "Inspirational creation" stresses the aesthetic effects of a good painting that derives from "association in thinking." A good painting should not only create a good image, but also enable the viewer to appreciate the underlying message. Such a painting is one of inspirational creation. "Association in thinking" and "inspirational creation" together constitute an inseparable process of artistic creation. This concept is the earliest definition of artistic conception and aesthetic appreciation in China; it later became an important principle underlying the theory on Chinese painting.

引例 Citations：

◎凡画，人最难，次山水，次狗马，台榭一定器耳，难成而易好，不待迁想妙得也。（顾恺之《论画》，见张彦远《历代名画记》卷五）

（凡是画画，画人最难，其次是画山水，再次是画狗马之类的动物，亭台楼榭是固定的器物，难画却容易画好，不需要迁想妙得。）

Painting human figures is most difficult; less difficult is painting the landscape, and then animals such as dogs and horses. Pavilions, which are fixed objects, are also difficult to paint, but it is easy to create accurate image of them because no inspirational creation based on association in thinking is required. (Gu Kaizhi: On Painting, as cited in Zhang Yanyuan: *Famous Paintings Through History*)

◎顾公运思精微，襟灵莫测，虽寄迹翰墨，其神气飘然在烟霄之上，不可以图画间求。（张怀瓘（guàn）《画断》，见张彦远《历代名画记》卷五）

（顾恺之运用心思精深微妙，他的襟怀与想法难以预料，虽然依托笔墨来表现，但他的神采气韵却高高飘于云霄之上，不能只在画面中寻求。）

Gu Kaizhi thought deeply before creating a painting, with his vision and thinking hard. His paintings were created through the use of ink and painting brushes, but his artistic appeal and charm have transcended his paintings, reaching high clouds. (Zhang Huaiguan: *An Appraisal of Paintings*, as cited in

Zhang Yanyuan: *Famous Paintings Through History*)

qīnqīn 亲亲

Affection for One's Kin

爱亲人，尤其是爱父母。"亲亲"既指一种自然的情感，同时也指这种情感在言行上的表现。儒家主张，应将对父母、对亲人的亲爱之情，推及他人，使之成为仁德的基础。但是，过度的"亲亲"，会导致行事上的偏私。因此，儒家提出了以"义"克服"亲亲"可能存在的局限。

This term refers to love for one's kin and particularly for one's parents. It is a natural affection, and it also refers to the way in which such feeling is expressed. Confucianism holds that such a love should also be extended to others so that it will foster public virtue. Excessive affection for one's kin, however, can lead to favoritism in one's conduct. So righteousness is proposed by Confucianism as a means to curb excessive love for one's kin.

引例 Citations：

◎亲亲，仁也；敬长，义也。无他，达之天下也。(《孟子·尽心上》)

(亲爱父母，是仁；尊敬兄长，是义。行善没有其他要求，就是将亲亲、敬长推之于天下之人。)

To love one's parents is benevolent; to hold one's elder brothers in reverence is righteous. Fostering virtue requires nothing but extending one's love for his kin to all the people in the world. (*Mencius*)

◎仁者人也，亲亲为大；义者宜也，尊贤为大。亲亲之杀（shài），尊贤之等，

礼所生也。(《礼记·中庸》)

(仁是人天生的本性，以亲亲为最重要的表现；义是行事合宜，以尊贤为最重要的表现。亲亲要有亲疏远近的不同，尊贤也要有差等，因此就产生了礼。)

Benevolence is the nature of man, which finds expression in one's love for his kin. Righteousness means doing the right thing on right occasions, which finds expression in one's respect for virtuous and visionary people. Love for one's kin and others should be extended in order of closeness of different relations, and the same should apply to respect to the virtuous and visionary people. This gives rise to rites. (*The Book of Rites*)

qīngmíng 清明

The Qingming Festival

中华民族四大传统节日（春节、清明节、端午节、中秋节）之一，是中国传统岁时体系中唯一与节气合一的节日，通常在 4 月 4 或 5 或 6 日。唐以前，清明主要作为二十四节气之一，反映自然时节的变化，与农事息息相关。唐宋以后，清明节取代寒食节而成为节日，寒食节原有的祭祖扫墓、吃冷食等成为清明节俗的内容。此时万物生气旺盛，人们顺应季节的变化，又有郊游踏青、插柳、放风筝、荡秋千等活动。时至今日，清明仍是中国人生活中具有特殊意义的节日。2006 年 5 月 20 日，经国务院批准，清明节被列入中国第一批国家级非物质文化遗产名录。

It is one of the four major traditional festivals, namely, the Spring Festival, the Qingming Festival, the Dragon Boat Festival and the Mid-autumn Festival, that are celebrated by the Chinese. It is the only Chinese festival which occurs on one of the solar terms of the traditional calendar, usually on April 4, 5 or 6. Prior to the Tang Dynasty, Qingming functioned primarily as one of the 24 solar terms that reflected natural changes of seasons and were closely associated with timing of agricultural activities. After the Tang and Song dynasties, Qingming took the place of the Hanshi ("Cold Food") Festival, and the practices of sweeping ancestral graves and eating cold food became prominent features of the Qingming Festival. At this time of year, with the coming of spring, all living things are bursting with vitality, and people go on country outings, plant willows, fly kites and play on swings. Today, Qingming has remained a festival of special significance to the Chinese. On May 20, 2006, it was included in the first batch of the National List of Intangible Cultural Heritage by the Chinese government.

引例 Citations：

◎清明时节雨纷纷，路上行人欲断魂。借问酒家何处有？牧童遥指杏花村。（旧题杜牧《清明》）

（清明时节下着纷纷小雨，路上的行人十分惆怅。向别人询问什么地方有酒家？牧童遥遥地指向杏花村。）

In the drizzling rain of Qingming, / A traveler walks with a heavy heart. / He asks, "Where can I find an inn?" / In response, a cowherd points to a village where apricot trees are in bloom. (Du Mu: Qingming)

◎燕子来时新社，梨花落后清明。（晏殊《破阵子》）

（燕子飞来的时候是春社，梨花飘落后就到了清明节。）

When the swallows return, it is the Spring Observance; / And after the pear blossoms fall, it is Qingming. (Yan Shu: Pozhenzi)

qióng zé biàn, biàn zé tōng, tōng zé jiǔ 穷则变，变则通，通则久

Extreme – Change – Continuity

事物达到极限则会发生变化，发生变化则能通顺，通顺则能长久。出自《周易·系辞下》，是对事物变化规律的一种认识。《系辞》认为，事物处于不断的变化之中，并且会在至极之时朝向对立面转化。人应把握这一事物变化规律，在穷极之时寻找变化的契机，促成事物的改变，以实现通顺而长久的发展。

When things reach their extreme, change occurs; after the change they evolve smoothly, and thus they continue for a long time. This notion comes from *The Book of Changes* and is a way of understanding the principles of change. According to this text, things are constantly changing and will, when they reach their extreme, develop in the opposite direction. People ought to understand the way of change, look for the turning point when things reach their extreme, and facilitate change so as to effect their smooth and long-lasting development.

引例 Citation：

◎《易》穷则变，变则通，通则久，是以"自天祐之，吉无不利"。(《周易·系辞下》)

(《易》揭示出，事物达到极限则发生变化，发生变化则能通顺，通顺则能长久，所以能够"从上天降下佑助，吉祥而无所不利"。)

The Book of Changes reveals that when things reach their extreme, change occurs. After the change they evolve smoothly, and thus they continue for a long time. That's how "Heaven bestows help to the human world and benefits all." (*The Book of Changes*)

qiútóng-cúnyì 求同存异

Seek Common Ground While Setting Aside Differences

寻求共同点，保留不同点。战国时期的学者惠施（前370？—前310？）、庄子（前369？—前286）等人认为，一切事物的差别、对立都是相对的，差异性中包含着同一性。从辩证的观点看，一切事物的差异都是相对的，都存在相互转化的可能。以孔子（前551—前479）为代表的儒家文化则强调在处理人与人、国与国之间关系时，在承认彼此有差异的前提下，通过协调而达到一种"和而不同"的状态。承认差异的存在或者暂时搁置差异，承认文化和价值观的多元，不追求绝对的一致、苟同，尽量站在对方的立场去看问题，努力寻求彼此的共同点，最终达成各方最大的共识。这一思想后来成为中国处理对外关系的重要理念。

The term means to seek points of agreement while maintaining difference of opinion. Scholars of the Warring States Period such as Hui Shi (370?-310? BC) and Zhuangzi (369?-286 BC) believed that differences and antitheses between all things are relative, and that commonalities exist within differences. From a dialectical perspective, differences between all things are relative and there is always the possibility of one thing transforming into its opposite. The Confucian culture represented by Confucius (551-479 BC) stressed that in relations between people and between states, "harmony without uniformity" should be achieved through accommodation, provided that differences between the parties are recognized. The greatest possible consensus between all sides is ultimately reached by acknowledging the existence of differences or setting them aside. To achieve such consensus, people should recognize the diversity of cultures and values and not seek absolute unanimity or forced agreement; and they should look at problems as much as possible from the perspective of others. This approach subsequently became an important principle underlying China's handling of foreign relations.

引例 Citations：

◎大同而与小同异，此之谓"小同异"；万物毕同毕异，此之谓"大同异"。(《庄子·天下》)

（大同小异与小同大异是有区别的，这种区别称为"小同异"；万物完全相同、完全不同，这称为"大同异"。）

When there are major commonalities and minor differences, or minor commonalities and major differences, it is called "minor commonality and differentiation." When things are totally identical or totally different, it is called "major commonality and differentiation." (*Zhuangzi*)

◎君子和而不同，小人同而不和。(《论语·子路》)

（君子与人和谐相处却不会盲目附和，小人盲目附和而不能真正和谐相处。）

A man of virtue pursues harmony but does not seek uniformity; a petty man seeks uniformity but does not pursue harmony. (*The Analects*)

sānxǐng-wúshēn 三省吾身

Reflect on Oneself Several Times a Day

多次反省自身。"三省吾身"是儒家所主张的一种道德修养方法。儒家认为，德行的确立取决于自身的追求与努力。因此应时时反省自己的言行与内心，并以此作为修养道德的基本方法。曾子（前 505—前 436）特别提出，每日应从尽己为人、诚信待人、温习课业等方面多次反省自身是否存在不足，有则改之，无则加勉。

Reflecting often on what one does – this is a way of self-cultivation of virtue advocated by Confucianism. This school of thought holds that as moral integrity is established with one's efforts of self-cultivation, one needs to constantly examine his words and deeds as well as what he has in mind as a fundamental way of improving himself. Zengzi (505-436 BC), in particular, stresses that one should everyday reflect many times on whether he has performed duties for others, treated others with good faith and whether he has reviewed what he learned to see if there is any room for improvement.

引例 Citation：

◎曾子曰："吾日三省吾身：为人谋而不忠乎？与朋友交而不信乎？传不习乎？"（《论语·学而》）

（曾子说："我每天多次反省自己：为他人谋划是否未尽心竭力？与朋友交往是否不守信诺？传授的学问是否没有温习？"）

Zengzi said: "Each day I reflect on myself several times: Have I tried all my best to help someone when offering advice to him? Have I kept my word to my friends? Have I reviewed what I learned?"(*The Analects*)

shàngbīng-fámóu 上兵伐谋

The Best Strategy in Warfare is to Foil the Enemy's Strategy.

用兵的上策是挫败敌方的计谋。是古代军事家孙武提出的一条军事原则。在孙武看来，军事斗争是在不同层面展开的。不同层面的斗争都可以对战争胜败产生重要的影响。其中，武力攻伐对于双方都会造成极大的伤害，因此是不得已的选择。善于用兵之人应在武力斗争发动之前，运用谋略破除敌人的进攻威胁，或为己方的武力攻伐扫清障碍，以最小的代价实现战略目标。

Foiling the enemy's strategy is an important principle proposed by Sunzi the ancient military strategist. In his view, war is waged at different levels, all of which have a significant impact on the outcome. Armed attacks will do great damage to both sides, so they should be avoided if at all possible. Those who are good at leading armies should be able to use stratagems to eliminate the threat of enemy attack in advance or clear the obstacles to their own armed forces to achieve their strategic goals at minimal cost.

引例 Citation：

◎故上兵伐谋，其次伐交，其次伐兵，其下攻城。攻城之法，为不得已。(《孙子·谋攻》)

（所以用兵的上策是挫败敌方的计谋，其次是破坏敌方的外交，再次是攻打敌方的军队，最下策是进攻敌方的城邑。攻城是不得已采取的办法。）

The preferred way is to foil the enemy's plans, the next best to use diplomacy, failing that to attack the enemy's forces, and the least desirable is to assault the enemy's cities. Assaulting cities is a last resort when all else has failed. (*The Art of War*)

shěshēng-qǔyì 舍生取义

Give One's Life to Uphold Righteousness

舍弃生命以保全道义。出自《孟子》。孟子（前372？—前289）认为，"义"是人之所以为人的本质特征之一，舍"义"而不足以为人。生命固然可贵，但生存却并不是人之所以为人的目的或意义。因此，当保全生命与坚守道义发生冲突的时候，人不应背义苟活，而应牺牲生命以捍卫道义。

This belief is advocated by Mencius (372?-289 BC). He holds that upholding righteousness is an essential attribute of a dignified man, and without it one would lose his moral standing. Life is precious, but survival should not be the only thing that is important in life. When one faces a choice between saving life and upholding righteousness, he should give life to uphold righteousness.

引例 Citation：

◎生亦我所欲也，义亦我所欲也，二者不可得兼，舍生而取义者也。(《孟子·告子上》)

（生命是我所渴望的，义也是我所渴望的，二者不能同时获得的时候，舍弃生命以保全道义。）

Both life and righteousness are important to me. However, if I cannot have both, I will give my life so as to uphold righteousness. (*Mencius*)

shěnyīn-zhīzhèng 审音知政

Assess Governance by Listening to Music

通过审察音乐了解一个国家的政治教化情况。是儒家文艺观的具体体现。儒家认为，乐为心声，能传达人的情感和感受，因此，国家政治是否清明、百姓生活是否富足、社会风气是否淳厚，往往会通过音乐表现出来。《左传》记载，春秋时期吴国公子季札出使鲁国，观赏鲁国人演奏的周代不同诸侯国或地区的音乐，并据此评析音乐中所反映出的各国治政状况。这应该是审音知政的源头。这一思想方式产生于秦汉时期，它打通了艺术和政治的界限，将艺术审美活动导向社会现实生活，体现出儒家文艺观以政教为本的特点，使中国古代文艺理论染上了浓郁的政治伦理色彩。

This term is an example of Confucian literary thinking. Confucian scholars believed that music gave expression to people's thinking and emotions, so a country's music reflected whether government integrity was upheld, whether people enjoyed prosperity, and whether the social atmosphere was amiable and sincere. According to *Zuo's Commentary on The Spring and Autumn Annals*, during his diplomatic mission to the State of Lu in the Spring and Autumn Period, Prince Jizha of the State of Wu learned about the governance of various vassal states and regions at the time by listening to their music performed by the people of Lu. This should be the origin of the term "assessing governance by listening to music." This concept first emerged in the Qin and Han dynasties, which removed the boundary between art and government and made artistic aesthetics a part of public life. It gave expression to Confucian literary thinking which was based on governance and ethics and added a political and ethical dimension to the ancient Chinese literary and art theory.

引例 Citations：

◎是故治世之音安以乐，其政和；乱世之音怨以怒，其政乖；亡国之音哀以思，其民困。声音之道，与政通矣。(《礼记·乐记》)

（所以，太平时代的音乐祥和欢乐，这是因为政治宽和的缘故；动乱时代的音乐充满了怨恨与愤怒，这是因为政治混乱的缘故；国家将亡时的音乐充满了悲哀忧思，这是因为民众困苦不堪的缘故。音乐所反映出的道理，与一个国家的政治是相通的。）

Hence, the music in time of peace indicates serenity and happiness because of good governance. The music in time of disorder indicates dissatisfaction and anger because of political turmoil. The music of a state on the verge of collapse reveals sorrow and anxiety because its people are in distress. So there is a connection between the music of a state and its governance. (*The Book of Rites*)

◎凡音者，生于人心者也。乐者，通伦理者也。是故知声而不知音者，禽兽是也。知音而不知乐者，众庶是也。唯君子为能知乐。是故审声以知音，审音以知乐，审乐以知政，而治道备矣。(《礼记·乐记》)

（凡是乐音，都是从人的内心产生。音乐则和社会的伦理相通。因此，知道声响但不懂得更高级乐音的，是禽兽。知道乐音但不懂得更高级音乐的，是众人。只有君子才能懂得音乐。因此，审察声响可以知晓乐音，审察乐音可以知晓音乐，审察音乐可以知晓一个国家的治政情况，如此则治理国家的方法就齐备了。）

All musical sounds come from human mind. Music is connected with social ethics. Therefore, those who know sounds but do not know the modulations are animals; those who know the modulations but do not know music are the common folk. Only men of virtue can really appreciate music. Therefore, one must examine sounds in order to know its modulations, and examine the modulations in order to know music. One must examine the music in order to assess governance. And so the way of governance is complete! (*The Book of Rites*)

shēngxiào 生肖

The Chinese Zodiac / Animal of the Year

也叫"属相"。中国古人把与农业生活相关的 11 种动物,加上特有的文化图腾"龙",与十二地支配合进行纪年,每个人出生的年份都有相对应的生肖动物,即十二生肖。十二生肖与十二地支的配合与排序如下:子鼠、丑牛、寅虎、卯兔、辰龙、巳蛇、午马、未羊、申猴、酉鸡、戌狗、亥猪。十二生肖至迟在东汉已经定型,成为中国民俗文化中富有特色的内容。直到今天,一个人的本命年、婚配、命运以及在剪纸等民间艺术里面,仍能看到生肖文化的身影。

Shengxiao (生肖) in Chinese refers to the twelve animals that make up the Chinese Zodiac. The ancient Chinese included in this list eleven animals closely associated with farming, plus the dragon, a legendary animal which has cultural symbolic meaning in China. They were then associated with the twelve Earthly Branches (in a twelve-year cycle) to each represent a year. Thus a person's year of birth is also associated with a specific animal. Combining the Zodiac with the Branches produces the following order: *zishu* (子鼠 rat), *chouniu* (丑牛 ox), *yinhu* (寅虎 tiger), *maotu* (卯兔 rabbit), *chenlong* (辰龙 dragon), *sishe* (巳蛇 snake), *wuma* (午马 horse), *weiyang* (未羊 sheep), *shenhou* (申猴 monkey), *youji* (酉鸡 rooster), *xugou* (戌狗 dog), and *haizhu* (亥猪 pig). The Zodiac had already entered into use by the Eastern Han Dynasty, and has been a distinctive feature of Chinese culture and folk tradition ever since. Today, the influence of the Chinese Zodiac culture can still be found in the tradition of a person's animal birth year, marriage and fortune-telling, and in folk arts, like paper-cutting.

引例 Citation：

◎昔在武川镇生汝兄弟，大者属鼠，次者属兔，汝身属蛇。(《周书·晋荡公宇文护传》)

(过去我住在武川镇，生下你们兄弟三人，老大属鼠，老二属兔，你属蛇。)

When I lived in the town of Wuchuan, you three brothers were born. The eldest is a Rat, the second a Rabbit, and you are a Snake. (*The History of Zhou of the Northern Dynasties*)

shínián-shùmù, bǎinián-shùrén 十年树木，百年树人

It Takes Ten Years to Grow Trees and a Hundred Years to Nurture Talents.

比喻栽培树木使之成材需要很长时间，培育人才则需要更长时间。其中的道理有两层：第一，培养和选拔人才关乎国家、社会的长远发展；第二，人才的培养和成长应立足于长远发展，要有战略眼光和整体规划，需作持久的努力。

This alludes to the long time it takes for a tree to grow, yet even longer time it takes to nurture talents. The implications are twofold: first, identifying and bringing up talents has long-term significance for the development of a country and a society; second, nurturing talents should be an undertaking pursued with strategic vision, sustained efforts and according to a comprehensive plan.

引例 Citation：

◎一年之计，莫如树谷；十年之计，莫如树木；终身之计，莫如树人。一树一获者，谷也；一树十获者，木也；一树百获者，人也。(《管子·权修》)
(做一年的打算，没有什么比得上种植庄稼；做十年的打算，没有什么比得上栽种树木；做一生的打算，没有什么比得上培育人才。一经种植而有一次的收获，是庄稼；一经栽种而有十倍的收获，是树木；一经培育而有百倍的收获，是人才。)

When planning for a year, there is nothing like growing crops; when planning for a decade, there is nothing like planting trees; when planning for a lifetime, there is nothing like nurturing talents. When you grow crops, you get one harvest; when you plant trees, you get a tenfold harvest; when you nurture talents, you get a hundredfold harvest. (*Guanzi*)

shí 时

Time / Timing

"时"有三种不同含义：其一，指天道运行的时序或规律，如春夏秋冬四时，或昼夜交替的时辰等。其二，指适宜于某种人事的天象或气候条件，如农时、天时等。其三，指人事发展过程中出现的时机、时运。"时"的出现与消失体现着天道或人事运行的规则。人应认识并把握"时"及其所体现的规则，采取与"时"相适应的行动。

Shi (时 time or timing) has the following three meanings: First, the sequence or rules of heaven's way, such as spring, summer, autumn, and winter; or hours that mark changes of time during day and night; Second, a certain celestial phenomenon or climatic condition having impact on human activity, such as seasons for farming or timing for other activities; Third, the right time or opportunity that emerges in the course of human activity. The emergence or disappearance of timing is governed by the rules of heaven's way or human behavior. People should gain a good understanding and master time or timing and their manifested rules and act in a way commensurate with them.

引例 Citations：

◎天何言哉，四时行焉，百物生焉，天何言哉？（《论语·阳货》）
（天何尝说话呢？四季周而复始，万物蓬勃生长，天又何尝说了什么呢？）

Has Nature ever said anything? The four seasons run their cyclical course and all things grow vigorously. Has Nature ever said anything? (*The Analects*)

◎时止则止，时行则行，动静不失其时。（《周易·彖下》）
（根据时势该静止就静止，该行动就行动，动静不错失时机。）

Stop what you do when timing is not right, act when timing is favorable. Move and stop as dictated by timing. (*The Book of Changes*)

shíxù 时序

Change Along with Times

即时世和时代变化。这一术语旨在揭示文学创作与时代变化的关系。南朝刘勰（465？—520）指出文学发展不是孤立的现象，而是受到时代多重因素的影响，包括当时的社会政治状况、统治者的个人爱好、学术思潮等。

The term suggests that literary creation is affected by changes of the times. Author and literary scholar Liu Xie (465?-520) of the Southern Dynasties who used this term pointed out that literary creation is not an isolated phenomenon. Rather, it is affected by numerous historical factors, such as the prevailing social and political conditions, the personal preferences of rulers, as well as intellectual trends.

引例 Citations：

◎ 故知歌谣文理，与世推移，风动于上，而波震于下者。(刘勰《文心雕龙·时序》)

（因此知道诗歌的文采情理随时代变化而变化，时政教化对诗歌的影响如同风在水面上吹，而水波就在下面震荡一样。）

Thus we know that songs and literary style change with the times, just like when the wind blows, waves are stirred up in the water. (Liu Xie: *The Literary Mind and the Carving of Dragons*)

◎ 文变染乎世情，兴废系乎时序。(刘勰《文心雕龙·时序》)

（文章的变化受到当世各种情况的影响，它的兴衰取决于时代的变化。）

Literary changes are affected by the ways of the world. A literary style's rise and decline in popularity is caused by changes of the time. (Liu Xie: *The Literary Mind and the Carving of Dragons*)

shǐ 史

History

在甲骨文与金文中,"史"的字形是手执笔或简簿,其义指记载史事的官吏。东汉许慎(58?—147)《说文解字》说:"史,记事者也。从又(手)持中。中,正也。""史"与"事"同源,记"事"的人叫"史",人所记叫"事"。后来史官所记述的史事或史实以及按一定原则编集整理的关于史事或史实的各种记载及评述也称作"史",即今之"历史"。按许慎说法,"史"字"从又持中",所谓"持中"就是坚持客观公正、无所偏袒的原则。中国有重史的传统,在很长时期内,史官甚至有不受当政者干涉的特殊地位。一方面,史家可以通过秉笔直书对当政者形成一定程度的制约,使其谨言慎行;另一方面,又可以通过总结、评述历史人物与历史事件汲取经验教训,为当政者提供借鉴。这一传统构成了中国人的人文精神和理性精神的重要特征。

In ancient inscriptions on tortoise shells and ox scapula, together with inscriptions on ancient bronze objects, the pictographic Chinese character *shi* (史) represents a hand holding a writing brush or a hand holding a bamboo slip, referring to a court official in charge of keeping historical records. *Explanation of Script and Elucidation of Characters* by Xu Shen (58?-147) in the Eastern Han Dynasty goes: "*Shi* is the person who keeps records of events. A hand in the middle implies maintaining justice." Same in sound, two differently-written Chinese characters *shi* (史 history) and *shi* (事 events) are from the same origin, and those who keep notes of what happens are called *shi* (史 record keeper) and what they write down is *shi* (事 records). Later, what the officials in charge of keeping records of historical incidents or events or collections of these incidents or events as well as comments about them are also called *shi* (史), which literally means history. According to Xu Shen, the original pictograph representing the Chinese character *shi* looks like a hand kept in the middle, which means keeping records of historical incidents or events objectively without lending favor to any side of an issue. Great emphasis was once placed on keeping records of history, and during certain periods, even the sovereign rulers were not allowed to interfere with the work of officials in charge of keeping records of historical incidents or events. On the one hand, by keeping records of historical incidents or events, such officials posed a deterrent to rulers, who had to be careful about what they said and what they did. On the other hand, by keeping records of or commenting on historical figures or events, lessons could be summed up or examples be set up, which rulers could draw on and learn from. This tradition constitutes an important aspect of Chinese people's humanistic and rationalistic spirit.

引例 Citations：

◎此人皆意有所郁结，不得通其道也，故述往事、思来者。(《史记·太史公自序》)

(这些人都是感情郁结，不能实现志向，所以记述往事，希望将来的人能够了解。)

They were depressed over what had prevented them from fulfilling their aspirations, so they wrote down what had happened in the hope that future generations would understand them. (*Records of the Historian*)

◎千古兴亡之理，得自简编；百王善恶之由，闻于经史。其间祸淫福善，莫不如影随形，焕若丹青，明如日月。(赵普《上太宗请班师》)

（自古以来国家兴亡的道理，从书中都能找得到；数百个帝王行善作恶的缘由，从经史记述中也都听说过。史籍中所记述的淫乱招致祸殃、行善得到福报的事情，都像影子跟随形体一样密不可分，像图画一样鲜明，像日月一样光亮。）

Reasons for the rise and fall of all states since antiquity can all be found in books; reasons why hundreds of emperors did good or evil deeds can also be read in classics and history books. The examples recorded of how licentiousness invited disasters and good deeds brought about fortune are omnipresent like our own shadows, and they are as obvious as the sun and moon and as evident as a painting. (Zhao Pu: Memorial Urging Emperor Taizong to Withdraw Troops)

shìwài-táoyuán 世外桃源

Land of Peach Blossoms / Land of Idyllic Beauty

晋陶渊明（365或372或376—427）在《桃花源记》中所描述的一个安乐而美好的地方。那里景色优美，与世隔绝，远离战乱，没有政治压迫，人们过着平等、自由、安宁、祥和、快乐而美好的生活。后喻指为人向往的美好世界或理想社会，也指脱离世俗、安乐自在的隐居之所。

In his essay "The Peach Blossom Spring," Tao Yuanming (365 or 372 or 376-427) of the Jin Dynasty describes an idyllic place of natural beauty, cut off from the outside world and far from the ravages of war, free from political oppression, where people live in equality, freedom, harmony, peace, and happiness. Later, the expression came to mean an imagined ideal society or place; also a refuge, away from material temptations where one could live in seclusion and tranquility.

引例 Citation：

◎土地平旷，屋舍俨然，有良田美池桑竹之属。阡陌交通，鸡犬相闻。其中往来种作，男女衣着，悉如外人。黄发垂髫（tiáo），并怡然自乐。（陶渊明《桃花源记》）

（眼前是平坦宽广的土地，房舍整整齐齐。有肥沃的田地、美丽的池沼和桑树竹林之类的景色。田间小路四通八达，鸡鸣狗叫都能听到。人们在田野里往来耕种劳作，男女的穿戴跟外人完全一样。老人和小孩个个都安适愉快，自得其乐。）

Before the eyes, the land lies wide and flat, dotted with neatly-built houses. There are fertile fields, picturesque ponds, and clumps of bamboo and mulberry trees. The paths in the fields branch in all directions, chickens cluck and dogs bark. People work in the fields, dressed in exactly the same manner as people outside. White-haired elders and tufted children alike seem happy and content. (Tao Yuanming: The Peach Blossom Spring)

suìhán-sānyǒu 岁寒三友

Three Friends of Winter / Steadfast, Loyal Friends

　　严寒时节的三位友人，具体指松、竹、梅三种植物。在中国传统文化中，有些植物因其自然属性而被赋予某种人文蕴涵。松、竹四季常青，历冬不凋；梅花凌霜傲雪，美丽绽放。三者都不怕严寒，在严寒中展现自身的生命力和自然美，宛如在严寒中相伴生长的好友，故被世人合称为"岁寒三友"。

它常被用来喻指忠贞不渝的友谊，寄托对于孤傲高洁人格的崇尚和向往。

"Three friends of winter" refer to the pine, bamboo and plum. In traditional culture, certain human characteristics are attributed to plants and animals based on their natural qualities. The pine and bamboo remain green all year round even in the coldest season, and the plum blooms in early spring when snow and frost are still frequent. These three plants are cold-resistant and retain their beauty even in harsh weather, just like good friends keep each other's company during an icy winter. This term is often used to refer to loyal and steadfast friendship, and also represent the fine qualities of high-mindedness and detachment.

引例 Citations：

◎岁寒，然后知松柏之后凋也。(《论语·子罕》)
（每年到了天气最寒冷的时节，才知道松树与柏树是最后凋谢的。）

Only when the year turns deadly cold do we see that pines and cypresses are the last to wither. (*The Analects*)

◎到深秋之后，百花皆谢，惟有松竹梅花，岁寒三友。(无名氏《渔樵闲话》第四折)
（到了深秋之后，各种花都凋谢了，只有松、竹、梅花依然生机盎然，是岁寒三友。）

By late autumn, all the other flowers have withered. Only the pine, bamboo and plum remain vibrant, thus described as three steadfast friends in the cold. (*Casual Talk Between a Fisherman and a Woodcutter*)

tāshānzhīshí, kěyǐ-gōngyù 他山之石，可以攻玉

Use Stones from Another Mountain to Polish One's Jade

别的山上的石头，可以用来琢磨玉器（"他"又作"它"）。语出《诗经》。本意是向周宣王（？—前782）委婉劝谏，应招致那些隐逸山林的贤才为国所用。后来比喻借他人的批评、帮助来改正自己的过错；借他人、他国的情况、经验、方法等作为自己的鉴戒和参考，更好地提升自我。它体现了中国人的开放心态、学习精神。

This expression, which is from *The Book of Songs*, was originally a subtle piece of advice to King Xuan of Zhou (?-782 BC) to recruit talented recluses to work for his country. Later, it became an allegory of using criticism from others to correct one's own mistakes, and drawing on the experiences and practices of other people or other countries to improve oneself. This phrase expresses the open-mindedness of the Chinese people and their eagerness to benefit from others' practices.

引例 Citation：

◎乐彼之园，爰有树檀，其下维榖（gǔ）。它山之石，可以攻玉。(《诗经·小雅·鹤鸣》)

（在那园中真快乐，檀树高高枝叶密，下面榖（chǔ）树矮又细。他方山上有佳石，可以用来琢玉器。）

The garden is so lovely, / Where tall sandalwood grows, / Below are short and slender mulberry trees. / There are stones on its rockeries, / Which can be used to polish jade. (*The Book of Songs*)

tiānlài 天籁

Sounds of Nature

天地万物自然发出的声音。庄子（前369？—前286）将声音分为"人籁""地籁"和"天籁"三种。"人籁"是人吹奏竹箫所发出的声音；"地籁"是风吹过大地上的孔洞所发出的声音；"天籁"并非是有别于二者的另一种声音，而是指天地万物自己所发出的千差万别的声音，并非他者有意使之发声。庄子对"天籁"的肯定，意在破除主观用心的影响，发现并尊重万物真实自然的状态。后人多用"天籁"指诗文天然浑成、得自然之趣的审美意境，用"天籁之音"指称自然发出的悦耳动听的乐声。

This term refers to sounds produced by all things in nature between heaven and earth. Zhuangzi (369?-286 BC) divided sounds into three categories: "human sounds," "terrestrial sounds," and "celestial sounds." According to him, "human sounds" refer to sounds made by a vertical bamboo flute when a person blows air into its top end. "Terrestrial sounds" refer to sounds produced by the earth's apertures when wind blows through them. "Celestial sounds" are not totally different from the above two. They refer to multifarious sounds made naturally by all things in the universe, which are not sounds created by external factors. By defining the "sounds of nature" this way, Zhuangzi meant to minimize the influence of the subjective mind so as to discover and respect the natural state of all things. People of later generations generally use this term to describe a literary work such as a poem or an essay that is written in a smooth way and has the appeal of natural charm. They also use the term "music of Nature" to refer to naturally produced sounds that are pleasant to the ear.

引例 Citation：

◎子游曰："地籁则众窍是已，人籁则比竹是已。敢问天籁。"子綦（qí）曰："夫吹万不同，而使其自己也，咸其自取，怒者其谁邪！"（《庄子·齐物论》）

（子游说："地籁是风吹过大地上的众多孔窍所发出的声音，人籁是人吹奏竹箫所发出的声音。请问天籁是什么？"子綦说："风吹过万种孔窍而使它们发出不同声音，这些声音都是各个孔窍的自然状态自己产生的，鼓动众窍发声的还有谁呢！"）

Ziyou said: "'Terrestrial sounds' are those produced by the earth's apertures; while 'human sounds' are those that come from a vertical bamboo flute. What then are 'celestial sounds'?" Ziqi answered: "When the wind blows across the land, it makes a myriad of different apertures produce varied sounds. Such sounds are made naturally by those apertures. What else could rouse them to create such sounds?" (*Zhuangzi*)

tuī'ēn 推恩

Extend Benevolence and Love

推广仁爱之心。"推恩"是孟子（前372？—前289）提出的一项对执政者的要求。孟子认为，每个人天生都具有对他者的仁爱之心。但仁爱之心需要不断扩充，才能成就现实的仁德。仁心的扩充是由近及远、由亲至疏的。对执政者而言，即是要发挥天生的仁爱之心，将自己对父母、子女的关爱，推及治下的百姓，这即是"推恩"。"推恩"是实现仁政的基本方式。

Mencius (372?-289 BC) advocated that those in power should govern with love and benevolence. He believed that humans by nature have love for their fellows, but that this needs to be widely inclusive in order to constitute a true rule with benevolence. Love and benevolence begin with close family and relatives but then should spread to embrace all the people under his rule. This is the way to achieve rule with benevolence.

引例 Citation：

◎故推恩足以保四海，不推恩无以保妻子。古之人所以大过人者，无他焉，善推其所为而已矣。(《孟子·梁惠王上》)
（因此推广仁爱之心，足以能够保有天下。不推广仁爱之心，不能保护自己的妻子和子女。古代的圣贤之所以能够在很大程度上超越常人，没有别的原因，只是善于推广他们的德行罢了。）

Therefore, extending love and benevolence will be able to maintain the rule of the whole country; without them even one's wife and children cannot be protected. The only reason ancient sages were able to surpass ordinary people was because they were able to expand the influence of their moral principles and conduct far and wide. (*Mencius*)

tuījǐ-jírén 推己及人

Put Oneself in Another's Place

以自己的心思推测别人的心思。亦即儒家所说的"恕道"，是实现仁民爱物的重要原则和方法。它首先承认人类在精神上的根本一致，进而以此为原点，弘扬宽和、仁爱精神，设身处地为他人着想，以自身的所思所欲去理解别人：自己不希望的，不要强加给别人；自己所希望的，也要帮助别人实现。

This term means to infer others' thoughts with one's own. It is exactly what Confucianism advocates as tolerance toward others, which is an important principle or method of caring for the people and cherishing all things. In the first place, such thinking believes that people basically share a common spirit. On this basis, tolerance and benevolence need to be advanced. One should show consideration for others by putting oneself in their place, and understand others by walking in their shoes. We should never do unto others what we would not want others to do unto ourselves, and whatever we would wish for ourselves, we should also help others to achieve.

引例 Citations：

◎他人有心，予忖度之。(《诗经·小雅·巧言》)
（别人有什么心思，我能揣测得到。）

We can guess how others feel by putting ourselves in their place. (*The Book of Songs*)

◎强恕而行，求仁莫近焉。(《孟子·尽心上》)
（努力按照将心比心的恕道去做，没有比这更接近仁的了。）

Nothing comes closer to benevolence than trying to empathize with others by standing in their shoes. (*Mencius*)

◎忠恕违道不远，施诸己而不愿，亦勿施于人。(《礼记·中庸》)
（忠和恕离大道不远，如果施加在自己身上而自己不愿意接受，那么也不要强加给别人。）

Loyalty and forgiveness is very close to the principle of integrity, which means we should never impose upon others what we are not willing to accept ourselves. (*The Book of Rites*)

xǐmù-lìxìn 徙木立信

Establish One's Credibility by Rewarding People for Moving a Log

通过让人搬动大木头（兑现赏金）来树立威信。据《史记》记载，商鞅（前390？—前338）变法之前，为了取信于民，命人在都城集市南门立一根三丈长的大木头，宣布无论是谁，只要把木头搬到集市北门，就会得到丰厚的赏金。有人壮着胆子做了，商鞅立刻赏了重金。人们由此确信商鞅说到做到，因而新法颁布后得以畅行无阻。其中最重要的是"立信"——取信于民：若要国家政令畅通无阻，首先必须取信，令出必行，这样才能得到百姓的支持和拥戴。

According to *Records of the Historian*, in order to gain the people's trust before initiating his political reforms, Shang Yang (390?-338 BC) announced that, regardless of whoever it might be, if anyone was able to move a huge log 3 *zhang* long (approx. 7 meters) from the southern gateway to the northern gateway of the market in the capital city, he would be amply rewarded. A person was bold enough to attempt this task and succeeded; hence he was immediately rewarded with a generous sum of money. After that, the people were convinced that Shang Yang was one who kept his word, and hence, he was able to issue his new decrees unimpeded. The important thing here is "the establishment of credibility" – winning the people's trust. In order to pass a country's decrees unimpeded, one must first gain trust, which is imperative for issuing a decree. Only in this way can the support and allegiance of the common people be gained.

引例 Citation：

◎令既具，未布，恐民之不信，已乃立三丈之木于国都市南门，募民有能徙置北门者予十金。民怪之，莫敢徙。复曰"能徙者予五十金"。有一人徙之，辄予五十金，以明不欺。卒下令。(《史记·商君列传》)
（法令已经完备，还没有公布，（商鞅）恐怕百姓不相信，于是在国都集市南门立了一根三丈长的大木头，向百姓招募，如果有人将木头从集市南门搬到北门，就赏给他十镒（yì，古人以一镒为一金，一镒相当于二十两或二十四两）黄铜（金钱）。百姓对此感到奇怪，没有人敢去搬木头。（商鞅）又宣布："谁能搬过去，就赏给他五十镒黄铜（金钱）。"有一个人将大木头搬到了集市北门，商鞅立即赏给他五十镒黄铜，以表明没有欺骗他。于是商鞅最终颁布了变法的命令。）

After the decrees for reform being drawn but before being issued, Shang Yang, fearing that the people wouldn't take the decrees seriously, he had a 3-*zhang*-long (approx. 7 meters) log erected in front of the southern gateway of the market place in the capital city. He declared that whoever could move the log from the southern gateway to the northern gateway would be given a reward of 10 *yi* (equivalent of 200 taels of copper). People found it very strange and nobody came forward to move the log. Shang then said, "Whoever can move the log will be awarded 50 *yi* (equivalent of 1,000 taels of copper)." One man came up and moved the log to the market's northern gateway. Shang kept his words and immediately gave him the promised amount of reward. Thus Shang was able to issue the decrees of reform thereafter. (*Records of the Historian*)

xiànsù-bàopǔ 见素抱朴

Maintain Originality and Embrace Simplicity

关注、保持素朴的状态。出自《老子》。"素"本指未经染色的丝,"朴"本指未经加工的木材,老子以"素、朴"指称人或事物未受外界干预时的自然状态。老子认为,执政者应摒弃有悖于人或事物自然本性的各种主张和诉求,引导百姓回复到素朴的自然状态。后用"见素抱朴"形容不为外物牵累、保持本真纯朴的秉性。

The term means to observe and maintain the natural state of things. This notion first appeared in the book *Laozi*. The original meaning of *su* (素) is undyed silk; *pu* (朴) is unworked wood or timber. Laozi used these terms as analogies for people and objects in their natural untouched state. He believed that those in power should not try to influence people or things with ideas or demands that run counter to their natural conditions. Instead they should guide the populace back to its simple, natural origin. The term later came to mean "be unaffected by external factors and retain its earliest, pure nature."

引例 Citation:

◎绝圣弃智,民利百倍;绝仁弃义,民复孝慈;绝巧弃利,盗贼无有。此三者,以为文不足,故令有所属,见(xiàn)素抱朴,少私寡欲。(《老子·十九章》)

(抛弃圣明与智慧,民众可以得到百倍的好处;抛弃仁义道德,民众恢复自然的孝慈;抛弃巧诈和货利,盗贼就会消失。圣智、仁义、巧利都是不必要的文饰,不足以治理天下,因此要使民众有所归属,保持素朴,减少私欲。)

Cast aside saintliness and wisdom, and the people will benefit greatly; cast aside benevolence and righteousness, and the people will revert to their natural dutiful feelings; cast aside smartness and gain and thieves will disappear. Saintliness and wisdom, benevolence and righteousness, and smartness and gain are all unnecessary embellishments and are inadequate for governance. People must return to their natural state and restrain their desire. (*Laozi*)

xiāosǎn-jiǎnyuǎn 萧散简远

Natural, Leisurely, Simple yet Profound

指书法、诗歌、文章等艺术作品的风格天然浑成、淡泊随意，而意蕴简古高远。"萧散"指自然闲适，没有刻意繁琐的修饰，不拘泥于法度规则。作为文艺批评术语，由宋代苏轼（1037—1101）提出，对明清时期的文艺创作与批评影响较大。它以庄子（前369？—前286）的思想为基础，又融入了禅宗的思想，强调自在散淡，心中不存执念，超越一切秩序与法度的羁绊，无往而不适，追求作品的疏朗、散淡、自由之美和合乎天然之趣。

This concept refers to those calligraphic works, poems, essays, and other literary and artistic works that are natural, leisurely and simple in style but have profound implications. A natural and leisurely style rejects excessive embellishment and is not bound by any particular forms. Created by Su Shi (1037–1101) in the Song Dynasty as a term of literary and art criticism, this concept had great influence on literary and artistic works in the Ming and Qing dynasties. Based on the thought of Zhuangzi (369?-286 BC) and including the thinking of the Chan Sect, this concept stresses the need to be leisurely and simple and the need to avoid being opinionated, to break free from the fetters of rules and regulations and to take things as they come to ensure that an artistic work embodies the beauty of leisure, simplicity, freedom, and naturalness.

引例 Citations：

◎予尝论书，以谓钟、王之迹，萧散简远，妙在笔画之外。至唐颜、柳，始集古今笔法而尽发之，极书之变，天下翕然以为宗师，而钟、王之法益微。至于诗亦然。（苏轼《书黄子思诗集后》）

（我曾经谈论书法，认为钟繇（yóu）、王羲之的书法，萧散简远，其妙处在笔画之外。到了唐代颜真卿、柳公权，集成古今的运笔方法而极力加以发挥，可以说穷尽了书法的变化，天下人一致推他们为宗师，钟繇、王羲之的书法影响反而越来越弱了。诗的创作也是这样。）

I once talked about calligraphy, and I said that the calligraphic works of Zhong You and Wang Xizhi were natural, leisurely, simple, yet profound, and their artistic appeal went far beyond the calligraphic works themselves. In the Tang Dynasty, Yan Zhenqing and Liu Gongquan drew on all the calligraphic styles of previous times to develop their own calligraphic styles. It is fair to say that Yan and Liu reached the zenith of calligraphic art, and they were unanimously regarded as the great calligraphic masters. In contrast, the influence of Zhong You and Wang Xizhi is on the decline. The same is true with poetry. (Su Shi: Postscript to *Selected Poems of Huang Zisi*)

◎诗至玄晖语益工，然萧散自得之趣，亦复少减，渐有唐风矣。（唐庚《书〈三谢诗〉后》）

（诗歌发展到谢朓（tiǎo），语句更加工整，但是自然闲适、悠然自得的趣味也随之减少了，逐渐有唐人作品的特点了。）

Xie Tiao's poems were more neatly done than his predecessors', but as a result such poems became less natural and leisurely, and one begins to see a distinctive feature of Tang poems in them. (Tang Geng: Postscript to *Poems of Xie Lingyun, Xie Huilian, and Xie Tiao*)

xīntóng-lǐtóng 心同理同

People of Similar Natures and Emotions Will Have Similar Understanding.

即"人同此心，心同此理"的简称。由南宋心学大家陆九渊（1139—1193）提出。陆王心学认为，人内在的心灵与外在的宇宙具有同等价值，真理是超越时空的，心和道是全人类共同的。只要是人，无论是古今东西，都会有同一的价值观念、同一的真理和道德认知，而人类认同的基础就在于此。明末清初之后，随着中西文化之间的大规模交流，心同理同这一观念被用来理解东西方学术文化上的共通与差异，认为西方舶来的异域新知虽然在形式上与中国既有的知识体系有差异，但根本思想是可以会通的。

The term, a shortened version of *ren tong ci xin, xin tong ci li* (人同此心，心同此理), was first proposed by Lu Jiuyuan (1139-1193). *Xinxue* (心学), the Neo-Confucian philosophy of Lu Jiuyuan and Wang Yangming (1472-1529), teaches that the innate knowledge of the human mind and the principles of the universe are in liaison, that truth transcends time and space, that the mind and the Dao are universal for all mankind. All human beings, past and present, east or west, have a common innate knowing of truth and morality, and this is the basis for a common human identity. As Western and Chinese cultures came into increasing contact after the Ming and Qing dynasties, this expression was an attempt to explain that, even though East and West differed in their academic cultures and much of the new knowledge differed in form from Chinese epistemology, their fundamental thinking could be reconciled.

引例 Citations：

◎千百世之上，有圣人出焉，此心同也，此理同也；千百世之下，有圣人出焉，此心同也，此理同也。（杨简《象山先生行状》）
（千百代之前，世上有圣人出现，他的心和理与我们现在是一样的；千百代之后，有圣人出现，那他的心和理与我们现在也是一样的。）

Ages ago, the sage's mind and reasoning were the same as ours today; generations later, the sage's mind and reasoning will be the same as ours today. (Yang Jian: Short Biography of Mr. Xiangshan)

◎且智慧既开以后，心理同而后起胜，自亦必有冥合古法之处，且必有轶过前人之处。（张之洞《劝学篇·外篇·会通》）
（况且智慧开启之后，天下之人人同此心，心同此理，而后兴起的要占优势，也肯定有暗合古法的地方，并且肯定有超越前人之处。）

When they begin to gain wisdom, people with similar natures and emotions will have similar understanding. Later knowledge will not only reflect the past, but will certainly also surpass it. (Zhang Zhidong: *Exhortation to Study*)

xīnyuè-chéngfú 心悦诚服

Be Completely Convinced and Follow Willingly

心中喜悦而诚心服从。"心悦诚服"是以德服人的结果或表现。孟子（前372？—前289）认为，令他人服从于自己，不能依赖于对他人的强制要求，而应通过提升自身的道德修养来实现。一个人如果具有崇高的品德，那么他者出于对德行的认同与喜悦，自然会服从于有德者在思想或政治上的主张。

This term means to gladly and willingly follow someone by virtue of their moral character and conduct. Mencius (372?-289 BC) believed that the proper way to convince others was not by forcing them to do something, but by demonstrating a high level of self-cultivation and morality. A person with high ethical standards will convince others, out of appreciation and regard, to accept his teachings or political ideas.

引例 Citation：

◎以力服人者，非心服也，力不赡也；以德服人者，中心悦而诚服也，如七十子之服孔子也。(《孟子·公孙丑上》)
（依靠强力使他人服从，他们并不是真心服从，而是力量不足以抗拒；通过德行而令人服从，他们是内心喜悦而诚心服从，就像是孔子的七十余位弟子钦服孔子那样。）

Coercion can bring people in line not because they are willing, but because they do not have the strength to resist; it is virtue that will persuade others to gladly and willingly follow, just as in the case of Confucius' more than seventy disciples who followed him out of true respect. (*Mencius*)

xìn 信

Good Faith

"信"的基本含义是恪守信诺、诚实不欺。"信"是为人立身需要遵守的基本道德。守信必须符合道义的原则，如果信约有悖于道义，则不能盲目追求信诺的履行。儒家特别强调两个方面的"信"：其一，是执政者应信守对百姓的承诺，百姓才会信服于政令。其二，是朋友之间应守信不欺。

This term means acting in good faith. Good faith is one of the principal ethical standards one should observe in order to establish oneself in society. However, one must comply with ethical principles in honoring a promise. If a promise goes against ethical principles, one should not blindly deliver it. Confucianism stresses the importance of acting in good faith for both rulers and people: A ruler must keep his promises made to the people so that they will abide by his decrees; one should be honest and truthful towards friends.

引例 Citations：

◎子曰："人而无信，不知其可也。大车无輗（ní），小车无軏（yuè），其何以行之哉？"(《论语·为政》)

(孔子说："人如果没有诚信，不知那怎么可以。就好像用牛拉的大车没有安装輗，用马拉的小车没有安装軏，它们怎么能够行驶呢？")

Confucius said: "How can an ox-drawn wagon be pulled if it has no yoke-bar, or a horse-drawn cart be pulled if it has no collar-bar? What good is a man if he acts without good faith?" (*The Analects*)

◎孟子曰："大人者，言不必信，行不必果，惟义所在。"(《孟子·离娄下》)
（孟子说："有德行的人，承诺不一定都信守，行为不一定都实行，只要是言行符合道义就行。"）

Mencius said: "A man of virtue does not have to keep all his promises or act as he says. What matters is that his words and deeds should conform to ethical principles." (*Mencius*)

xíngjù-shénshēng 形具神生

Physical Form Gives Birth to Spirit.

人的形体具备以后精神活动随之产生。"形"指人的形体，"神"指包括情感、意识在内的各种精神活动。荀子（前313？—前238）提出，人的形体和精神，与万物一样，都是在天道的运行中自然生成的。人的形体先于精神而生成，形体的具备构成了精神产生的条件。人的精神依存于形体之中。

When a person's physical form has fully developed, he will develop spiritual activity accordingly. Here "form" refers to the physical form of a human being, and "spiritual" refers to various mental activities, including emotions and consciousness. Xunzi (313?-238 BC) pointed out that a person's physical form and spirit, just like everything else, develop naturally in the course of the movement of the way of heaven. Spirit is born in the wake of physical formation of a human being. Full physical form is a prerequisite to the birth of spirit. A person's spirit exists within his physical form.

引例 Citation：

◎天职既立，天功既成，形具而神生。好恶、喜怒、哀乐藏焉，夫是之谓天情。(《荀子·天论》)
(天的职能已经确立，天的功效已经实现，人的形体具备了，人的精神活动也随之产生。好恶、喜怒、哀乐等情感蕴藏在形体之中，这就叫做天然的情感。)

When the functions of Nature have been established and brought into play, one's physical form emerges and his spirit is born. Love and hatred, delight and anger as well as grief and joy all develop within one's physical form; and they are called natural emotions. (*Xunzi*)

xìngfèn 性分

Natural Attribute

万物的本性所规定的内容与限度。郭象（？—312）提出，每个人或每一事物都有各自的本性，且本性有着具体的内容与限度，如事物的大小、形状，人的年寿、智愚等。人和事物的本性是天生所具、不得不然的，因此也是不能改变的。万物都应该安于自身的"性分"。人和事物如果能够按照本性的要求，在"性分"的范围内活动行事，就是自由、逍遥的。

This term refers to the features and limitations determined by the intrinsic nature of all things. Guo Xiang (?-312), a scholar in the Western Jin Dynasty, pointed out that each person or object has his or its own intrinsic natural attributes, such as size and shape of an object, or the life expectancy and intelligence or lack of it of a person. The natural attributes of a person or an object are inborn and therefore unchangeable. All things should remain content with their natural attributes. If people and objects follow their own nature and act within the scope of their natural attributes, they can enjoy unhindered freedom of movement.

引例 Citation：

◎天性所受，各有本分，不可逃，亦不可加。（郭象《庄子注》卷二）
（人和事物所禀受的天性，各有各的内容与限度，不能够逃避，也不能够改变。）

People and objects each have their own natural attributes and limitations, which they cannot ignore or alter. (Guo Xiang: *Annotations on Zhuangzi*)

xiūyǎng-shēngxī 休养生息

Recover from a Social Upheaval and Restore Production / Develop Economy and Increase Population

休息保养，繁殖人口。指在战争或社会大动荡之后，执政者减少徭役和征税，重视农业发展，减轻人民负担，安定人民生活，恢复社会元气。"休养生息"作为治国方略，产生于汉初，时历秦末战乱，民生凋敝，百废待举，它有效恢复了国家和社会的元气。自此之后，"休养生息"作为一种重要的治国理念和政策，贯穿于中国历史的不同时期，或是执政者迫于社会现实不得已而为之，或是出于让民众休息的仁政实践，或是两者兼而有之。这一政策是"民惟邦本"理念的具体体现。

The term means that in a period of peace after war or social upheaval, the economy and population can recover and multiply. In practice it means the sovereign shall reduce taxes and conscript labor, support agriculture, allowing the population to procreate, life to return to normal, and society to recover. It first appeared as a governing strategy in the early Han Dynasty after the ravages of the wars with the previous Qin Dynasty. By the time the Han took over, the country was devastated and the population severely depleted. This policy allowed society to gradually recover and the nation to grow. From then on, "develop economy and increase population" became an important principle and policy of government throughout Chinese history. Sometimes it was instituted reluctantly because of specific circumstances, sometimes actively pursued as a manifestation of benevolent rule, sometimes a mixture of both. It is the concrete application of the social and political principle that "people are the foundation of the state."

引例 Citations：

◎汉兴，扫除烦苛，与民休息。至于孝文，加之以恭俭，孝景遵业，五六十载之间，至于移风易俗，黎民醇厚。(《汉书·景帝纪赞》)
（汉朝建立后，废除秦朝制定的一切繁琐严苛的政令，让民众休养生息。到汉文帝之时，奉行恭谨俭约的政策，景帝承继了这一做法，五六十年之间社会风俗就得到了很大改善，百姓都变得朴实敦厚了。）

In the early days of the Han Dynasty, rulers abolished numerous harsh laws of the former Qin Dynasty, giving the people time to recover and multiply. Emperor Wen of Han carried out respectful, cautious, and thrifty policies that were continued by Emperor Jing. Thus after fifty to sixty years of such rule, social atmosphere improved, and the people became decent and honest. (*The History of the Han Dynasty*)

◎［霍］光知时务之要，轻徭薄赋，与民休息。(《汉书·昭帝纪赞》)
（霍光懂得当前国家重大事情的关键在于减轻徭役、降低赋税，让民众休养生息。）

Huo Guang understood that what the state needed most was to give time for the population to recover and multiply by lightening taxes, and cutting back on conscript labor. (*The History of the Han Dynasty*)

xiūcí-lìchéng 修辞立诚

Establish Credibility Through Careful Choice of Words

　　修撰文辞，确立诚信。"修"指修撰、修饰，也有人认为指内心的修养省察。"辞"指言辞、文辞，是所说的话语；也有人认为指文治教化。"立"，建立，确立。"诚"是诚信，包含文辞真实、内容信实、感情诚挚、恭敬守信等多重含义。因文字训诂的不同及对"修辞""立诚"二者关系的认识不同，对"修辞立诚"的含义主要有两种理解：其一，整顿礼乐法度，确立诚信。意思是治国者要以诚信之心撰写文辞，将自己的治国原则和规范注入其中；通过文辞的表达、传播，使这种原则和规范在民众中得以确立，并内化为人们的诚信品格。"立诚"是"修辞"的出发点，也是"修辞"的最终归宿。其二，撰写文章要表达作者真实的思想情感，不可浮文虚饰。儒家认为，文辞是传达思想感情的，思想感情、道德品质的差异，必然最终表现为文章的优劣。无论作何解释，"修辞立诚"都反映出中国人对于名实相副、言行一致、表里如一等诚实、诚信品格的崇尚。

This term means to establish credibility by careful use of language. The Chinese character *xiu* (修) refers to the careful selection of words and phrases as well as logical arrangement of text in writing a story, and some believe that it also refers to the cultivation of one's mind. The Chinese character *ci* (辞) refers to what one says, and some interpret it as governance of public affairs and cultivation of good manners. The Chinese phrase *licheng* (立诚) means to establish credibility. When it comes to the writing of stories, it means what one writes about is true, the rhetoric one uses is plain and simple and one is sincere in expressing his or her feelings. Because of different written explanations in ancient books as well as different interpretations about the relationship between *xiuci* and *licheng*, this set phrase has primarily two meanings. The first addresses the overhaul of rituals and music as well as legal codes. This means that rulers must compose documents or essays with sincerity so that the principles for governance and social norms can be explicitly illustrated in documents or essays. As a result, the principles for running the country and social norms will be accepted by the public from well-written documents and essays, and be followed to the letter. The second refers to the expression of what a writer really thinks and feels when it comes to the writing of stories or essays. Confucianism holds that diction conveys what a writer thinks and feels, and hence the moral integrity of the writer can find expression in what he writes. If anything, this phrase indicates the importance Chinese people attach to the consistency between language and reality, between one's words and actions, and between one's appearance and inner thoughts.

引例 Citation：

◎君子进德修业。忠信，所以进德也。修辞立其诚，所以居业也。(《周

易·文言》)

(君子要不断增进美德，修成功业。为人忠实守信，可以增进美德。修撰文辞，确立诚信，可以积累功业。)

A man of virtue should never stop promoting virtue and seeking improvement. Being honest and trustworthy helps in strengthening the cultivation of virtue. Establishing credibility by cultivating diction can lead to the accumulation of achievements. (*The Book of Changes*)

xiūdé-zhènbīng 修德振兵

Cultivate Virtue and Strengthen the Army

修养德行而整顿军队。"修德"指执政者修养自身的德行，并按照道德的原则施行政事，安顿百姓。"振兵"即整顿军队、提升军力。但"振兵"的目的不在于以强大的武力威胁他人、谋取利益，而是要在道德的规范下，保持足够的武力以维护社会的秩序与百姓的利益，在"修德"的基础上，合理运用武力。

Those in power should cultivate their own virtue, thus improving their moral character, conduct government affairs according to moral principles, and arrange for the people to live in peace. Strengthening the army means enhancing military might through training and discipline. However, the aim is not to threaten others with overwhelming might to obtain advantages but to maintain sufficient strength under moral standards to safeguard social stability and the interests of the people, using armed strength in a reasonable way on the basis of "cultivating virtue."

引例 Citation：

◎轩辕乃修德振兵，治五气，蓻（yì）五种，抚万民，度四方。(《史记·五帝本纪》)

（轩辕黄帝修养德行、整顿军队，研究五行之气的变化，种植五谷，安抚百姓，丈量四方土地而加以规划。）

The Yellow Emperor cultivated virtue and strengthened the army; he studied the changes of the five elements (metal, wood, water, fire, and earth), grew the five kinds of grain, reassured the people, surveyed the land and planned its use. (*Records of the Historian*)

xuándé 玄德

Inconspicuous Virtue

隐晦而不彰显的德行。道家将"玄德"作为统治者的至高品德。道家认为，"道"作为万物的本原，其基本内容是以"无为"的方式顺应并发挥万物的本性。而"玄德"即是统治者效法于"道"的具体表现。"玄德"要求统治者在为政中节制自己所掌握的权力，避免对百姓的干预，顺应、保全百姓的自然状态。

This term refers to moral conduct that is discreet and unobtrusive. The Daoists believe this is the highest manifestation of morality in a ruler. Dao is the source of all beings and things, and is manifested through *wuwei* (无为) or non-action. By being discreet and unobtrusive in his moral conduct, the ruler thus emulates Dao. *Xuande* (玄德) requires the ruler to exercise restraint in his use of authority to avoid interfering with the natural state of his people, which he should comply with and maintain.

引例 Citation：

◎道生之，德畜之，物形之，势成之。是以万物莫不尊道而贵德。道之尊，德之贵，夫莫之命而常自然。故道生之，德畜之，长之育之，成之熟之，养之覆之。生而不有，为而不恃，长而不宰。是谓玄德。(《老子·五十一章》)（道生成万物，德蓄养万物，万物呈现各自的形态，环境使万物成长。所以万物没有不尊崇道而珍贵德的。道之所以受尊崇，德之所以被珍贵，就在于它不施加命令而常顺应万物的自然状态。因此道创生万物，德蓄养万物，长养培育万物，成就万物，养护万物。创生万物而不据为己有，影响万物而不自恃己能，养育万物而不为主宰，这就是玄德。）

Dao is the origin of all things; virtue nurtures all things, which thus assume their different forms, and grow in different environments. That is why all things and beings revere Dao and cherish virtue. This reverence and cherishing arise because there are no demands imposed on the natural state of things and beings. Instead this state is respected. Thus Dao creates all things, virtue nurtures them, and the environment makes them grow and mature. Create without possessing, influence without showing off one's ability, and cultivate without controlling. Such is the quality of inconspicuous virtue. (*Laozi*)

xuánliáng-cìgǔ 悬梁刺股

Tie One's Hair on the House Beam and Jab One's Side with an Awl to Keep Oneself from Falling Asleep while Studying

"头悬梁，锥刺股"的略语。字面意思是把头发拴在屋梁上，用锥子扎大腿。来源于古人刻苦读书的故事。东汉的孙敬经常关起门，独自一人从早到晚不停读书。疲倦和劳累时就将头发拴在屋梁上，只要一低头，头发就被拉住，人马上清醒，再接着读。战国时代的苏秦（？—前284），每当困乏欲睡的时候，就用锥子扎自己的大腿，以保持头脑清醒，继续苦读。后人常以这两个故事鼓励年轻人发愤读书，努力学习。今天，这种有损身体健康的极端方式已不再提倡，但其刻苦求知的精神仍广为称颂。

The term literally means to tie one's hair on the house beam and jab one's side with an awl. The idiom comes from the ancient story about how assiduously people studied. Sun Jing of the Eastern Han Dynasty would incessantly read books from dawn to dusk alone. When he felt tired or fatigued, he would tie his hair to the beam of the house, so that the moment he began to nod off, his head would be jerked back and this would immediately rouse him, and he could continue reading. During the Warring States Period, Su Qin (?-284 BC) would use an awl to jab at his own thigh whenever he felt sleepy, to make sure he stayed awake and lucid enough to be able to continue reading. Later, people started to tell these stories in order to encourage young people to study hard. Today, this kind of extreme measures which are physically harmful are no longer encouraged. However, this kind of assiduous spirit in the pursuit of knowledge is still highly lauded.

引例 Citation：

◎头悬梁，锥刺股。彼不教，自勤苦。(《三字经》)
（孙敬读书时把头发拴在屋梁上［以免打瞌睡］；苏秦读书，［每到困倦时就］用锥子扎大腿。他们不用别人督促，而是自觉地勤奋苦读。）

Sun Jing tied his hair to a roof beam to prevent himself from falling asleep while reading; Su Qin jabbed at his own thigh with an awl to keep himself from dozing off while studying. They both studied hard on their own initiative without other's supervision. (*Three-character Classic*)

yán bì xìn, xíng bì guǒ 言必信，行必果

Promises Must Be Kept; Actions Must Be Resolute.

说话一定要有诚信，做事一定要果断。语出《墨子》与《论语》。墨家与儒家都赞成一个人说话应讲诚信，做事应当果敢，言行必须一致。但是孔子（前551—前479）与孟子（前372？—前289）对"言必信，行必果"提出了更高的要求，即统治者需要言而有信、取信于民，才能得到百姓拥戴，百姓才敢于说出真话。但在现实中不可以一味固守"言必信，行必果"，而应当遵从道义的需要，在符合道义的前提下权衡利弊，根据具体情况而作适当变通。后世在运用这一术语时，多强调一个人应当讲诚信，做事果断，能兑现承诺并且言行一致。

The expression comes from *Mozi* and *The Analects*. Followers of Mozi and Confucian ethics admired those who could keep their promises and whose actions were resolute. They believed speech and action should match. However, Confucius (551-479 BC) and Mencius (372?-289 BC) took this further to apply to rulers who, only by being as good as their words and trustworthy in their speech, could earn the confidence and support of their subjects who, in turn, would be truthful with them. For Confucius, this principle, rather than be followed too rigidly, should in practice be applied on the basis of what is ethical under specific conditions and after careful weighing the pros and cons. Later, the expression came to refer to honest speech and firm action, keeping one's word, and also "suit action to word."

引例 Citations：

◎言必信，行必果，使言行之合，犹合符节也，无言而不行也。(《墨子·兼爱下》)

(说出的话一定要守信用，做事一定要果断，使说的和做的能够像符节一样吻合，说出的话没有一句不去落实的。)

Promises must be kept; actions must be resolute. They should fit together like the two parts of a tally stick: everything said must be put into practice. (*Mozi*)

◎言必信，行必果，硁（kēng）硁然小人哉！抑亦可以为次矣。(《论语·子路》)

(说话一定守信，行动一定果断，这是固执而不知变通的一般人！但也可以算得上次一等的士了。)

Always keeping one's word without forethought is the sign of an obstinate and stubborn person, but he can still be considered a gentleman of a second degree. (*The Analects*)

◎大人者，言不必信，行不必果，惟义所在。(《孟子·离娄下》)

(有德行的人，承诺不一定都信守，行为不一定都实行，只要是言行符合道义就行。)

A man of virtue does not have to keep all his promises or act as he says. What matters is that his words and deeds should conform to ethical principles. (*Mencius*)

yīyán-xīngbāng 一言兴邦

A Single Remark Makes a Country Prosper.

一句话而使国家兴盛。治国理政是一项复杂的工作，不可能通过简单地依循一句话所表述的某个具体要求，就实现国家的兴盛。但如果执政者能够充分意识到治理天下的困难，并因此在为政中谨言慎行，始终不懈怠，那么凭借为政者的这种观念，则可能实现国家的兴盛。这种观念的作用即接近于"一言兴邦"。

A single remark can help a country thrive. As governance is a highly complex undertaking, it is impossible to make a country prosperous simply by following an idea expressed in a single remark. However, if a ruler thoroughly understands how difficult it is to run a country and exercises governance with prudence and dedication, it is quite possible for him to make his country prosper. In this sense, the effect of such concept, which can almost be likened as a single remark, will make a country flourish.

引例 Citation：

◎定公问："一言而可以兴邦，有诸？"孔子对曰："言不可以若是其几（jī）也。人之言曰：'为君难，为臣不易。'如知为君之难也，不几乎一言而兴邦乎？"（《论语·子路》）

（鲁定公问："一句话就可以使国家兴盛，有这回事吗？"孔子回答说："不可以对一句话有这样的期待。人们说：'做君主难，做大臣也不容易。'如果君主懂得做君主的艰难，不也就近乎一句话而使国家兴盛了吗？"）

Duke Ding of the State of Lu asked: "Is there a single remark that can make a country thrive?" Confucius replied: "No single remark can be expected to perform such a deed. There is a saying: 'It is not easy to be a ruler, nor is it easy to be a court official.' However, a ruler who truly understands how hard it is to govern a country will have a vision, which is almost like a single remark, and that will make his country prosper." (*The Analects*)

yīyǐguànzhī 一以贯之

Observe a Fundamental Principle Throughout One's Pursuit

用一个根本性的原则贯通学问、行事的始终。贯：贯通，统摄。按照儒家的要求，立身处事需要掌握多方面的知识和技能，遵守各种道德与礼法的规范。而孔子（前551—前479）强调，这些看似繁复的知识、技能与规范，贯穿着一个根本性的原则。孔子引导学生去认识、把握这一原则，并以此统摄学问、行事中的各种具体要求。后世学者对这一根本性的原则究竟为何有不同的解释，曾子（前505—前436）认为就是"忠恕"之道。

One needs to observe a fundamental principle in the entire process of academic and other pursuits. According to Confucianism, to establish oneself, one should gain a good command of knowledge and skills in a wide range of areas and abide by moral principles and norms. Confucius (551-479 BC) himself stressed that there is a fundamental principle running through all such knowledge and skills as well as moral standards. He taught his disciples how to master this fundamental principle so as to meet the requirements for doing things with knowledge and skills acquired. Scholars of later generations have different interpretations about what this fundamental principle is. Zengzi (505-436 BC) believed that it is loyalty and forbearance.

引例 Citations：

◎子曰："参（shēn）乎！吾道一以贯之。"曾子曰："唯。"子出，门人问曰："何谓也？"曾子曰："夫子之道，忠恕而已矣。"(《论语·里仁》)

（孔子说："曾参呀！我的学说贯穿着一个根本性的原则。"曾子说："是。"孔子出去后，其他弟子问曾子："是什么意思呢？"曾子说："老师的学说，只是忠和恕罢了。"）

Confucius said: "Zeng Shen, there is one thing that runs through my doctrine." Zengzi said: "Yes." When Confucius went out, other disciples asked him: "What did he mean?" Zengzi said: "Confucius' doctrine is simply this: loyalty and forbearance." (*The Analects*)

◎子曰："赐也，汝以予为多学而识之者与（yú）？"对曰："然。非与？"曰："非也，予一以贯之。"(《论语·卫灵公》)

（孔子说："端木赐，你以为我是个学了很多而又能够记得住的人吗？"子贡回答说："对啊，难道不是吗？"孔子说："不是的，我用一个根本性的原则来贯穿它们。"）

Confucius said: "Duanmu Ci (styled Zigong), you think I have learned a lot and am able to remember them all, do you?" Zigong replied: "Yes. Don't you think so too?" Confucius said: "No, what I have done is to master a fundamental principle that runs through them all." (*The Analects*)

yǐnshuǐ-sīyuán 饮水思源

When Drinking Water, One Must Not Forget Its Source.

喝水的时候，要想到水是从哪里来的。南北朝时，庾信（513—581）被迫在北朝客居二十多年，他常常思念故土，写文章说自己喝到河里的水就想到水的源头，以此抒发对于南朝的情怀。后世将原文约为"饮流怀源"或"饮水思源"，比喻不忘本、知感恩。这种纯良的品格，历来为人称道。

When drinking water, one should not forget its source. During the Southern and Northern Dynasties, Yu Xin (513-581) was forced to leave home and stay away from his home state for more than 20 years. Often homesick, he wrote in one of his essays that he always thought of the source of the water whenever he drank from the river, expressing his longing for his hometown in the Southern Dynasties. Eventually this became an idiom: when drinking water one should think of its source, implying that one should never forget his origin and always be grateful. This virtue has always been highly praised.

引例 Citation：

◎落其实者思其树，饮其流者怀其源。（庾信《徵调曲》其六）
（采食树上结的果实，便想到了结果实的树；喝到河中的水，便想到了河水的源头。）

When eating fruits I think of the fruit trees; when drinking water I think of the source of the river. (Yu Xin: The Tune of Zhi)

yǒng 勇

Courage

"勇"的基本含义是勇敢。"勇"作为一种德行,要求在行事之时,不畏惧困难,不计较个人利害,始终坚守道义的原则,敢于制止违背道义的行为。"勇"的表现需要基于对道德、礼法的认知与遵守。如果缺少对道德、礼法的遵守,勇敢之行就会流于好勇斗狠或铤而走险,并导致社会混乱。

The basic meaning of *yong* (勇) is courage, which is a virtue. When necessary, a courageous person is expected to fearlessly stop any act that violates ethical principles without giving any consideration to his own personal interests. Acts of courage must be based upon recognition and observance of ethical and social norms. Otherwise, such acts may become ruthless, brutal and risky, and cause social chaos.

引例 Citations:

◎子曰:"非其鬼而祭之,谄也。见义不为,无勇也。"(《论语·为政》)
(孔子说:"不是自己应该祭祀的鬼神而去祭祀它,是谄媚。遇见合乎道义的事却没有作为,是无勇。")

Confucius said: "One who offers sacrifices to other people's ancestors is a flatterer. One who knows what is right but takes no action is lacking in courage." (*The Analects*)

◎子路曰:"君子尚勇乎?"子曰:"君子义以为上。君子有勇而无义为乱,小人有勇而无义为盗。"(《论语·阳货》)

（子路说："君子崇尚勇敢吗？"孔子说："君子以道义为最崇高的要求。君子只有勇敢而不守道义就会作乱，小人只有勇敢而不守道义就会当盗贼。"）

Zilu asked: "Should a person of virtue act with courage?" Confucius answered: "A man of virtue should observe ethical principles above everything else. One who has courage but ignores ethical principles will become a trouble maker. A petty person who has courage but ignores ethical principles will become a thief or a robber." (*The Analects*)

yúgōng-yíshān 愚公移山

The Foolish Old Man Who Moved the Mountains

比喻有恒心和毅力，敢于知难而进。出自《列子·汤问》，是中国古代著名的寓言故事。愚公年近九十，门前正对大山，出门需绕行很远。为了不受大山阻隔，他终年率子孙凿山移石，遭智叟嘲笑而不放弃，终于感动天帝派天神移走了大山。在历史语境中，它蕴含着对于愚与智、有限与无穷、人力与自然力、人道与天道关系的思考。唐宋以降，寓言中勇于面对和挑战困难并且持之以恒的内涵被发掘，自此"愚公移山"成为迎难而上、坚持不懈的代名词。

This famous ancient Chinese fable from *Liezi* extols perseverance, determination and eagerness to surmount difficulty. Two huge mountains lay directly in front of the Foolish Old Man's house. The Foolish Old Man, who was almost ninety years old, had to take a long detour whenever he went out. To get rid of this inconvenience, he led his sons and grandsons in chipping away at the mountains year after year. They would not give up despite jeers of the Wise

Old Man, and eventually moved God, who sent heavenly spirits to move the mountains away. Originally, this fable pondered the relationship between foolishness and wisdom, the finite and the infinite, the forces of humans and the forces of nature as well as the relationship between the way of humans and the way of heaven. Since the Tang and Song dynasties, however, its underlying message about courage and perseverance in the face of challenge and adversity has gained increasing appreciation. Since then, the "Foolish Old Man Who Moved the Mountains" has become a synonym for forging ahead in the face of difficulties and persevering to the very end.

引例 Citations：

◎河曲智叟笑而止之，曰："甚矣，汝之不惠！以残年余力，曾（zēng）不能毁山之一毛，其如土石何？"北山愚公长息曰："汝心之固，固不可彻，曾不若孀妻弱子。虽我之死，有子存焉；子又生孙，孙又生子；子又有子，子又有孙；子子孙孙无穷匮也，而山不加增，何苦而不平？"（《列子·汤问》）（河曲智叟嘲笑并阻止愚公说："你太不聪明了！就凭你在这世上最后的几年和剩下的这点儿力气，还不能毁掉山上的一根草木，能把这大山的土石怎么样呢？"北山愚公长叹了一口气说："你的脑子太顽固，顽固得不开窍，连寡妇、孤儿都比不上。即使我死了，还有我儿子在呀；儿子又生孙子，孙子又生儿子；儿子又有儿子，儿子又有孙子；子子孙孙永无穷尽，可是这两座山却不会再增高了，还愁什么挖不平呢？"）

The Wise Old Man of the River Bend laughed at the Foolish Old Man and tried to stop him, saying, "You're really too foolish! With the few years and little strength that you still have, you wouldn't even be able to fell a tree on the mountain. How can you possibly move all the soil and rocks?" The Foolish Old Man of the North Mountain heaved a long sigh and said, "You are so pigheaded! Even widows and orphans know better. It is true that I will die, but my sons will survive and they will have sons. Then their sons will have sons, and those sons will also have sons, and I will have endless sons and grandsons, but these two mountains will grow no higher. Why can't they be leveled?" (*Liezi*)

◎精卫填海、愚公移山，志之谓也。（杨亿《处州龙泉县金沙塔院记》）

（精卫填海和愚公移山，讲述的都是立志。）

The tales of the mythical bird Jingwei filling in the ocean and of the Foolish Old Man moving the mountains are about determination. (Yang Yi: A Record of the Jinsha Temple in Longquan County, Chuzhou Prefecture)

◎各奋愚公之愿，即可移山；共怀精卫之心，不难填海。（蔡锷《劝捐军资文》）

（大家如果都立下愚公那样的志向，就可以搬走大山；人们都怀抱精卫那样的雄心，填平大海也不再困难。）

If everyone has the determination of the Foolish Old Man, we can move mountains; if we have the ambition of Jingwei, it will not be hard to fill in the ocean. (Cai E: A Call for Donations to the Army)

yǔshí-xiéxíng 与时偕行

Go with the Times

行事之法与"时"一起变化。出自《周易·彖下》。"时"即时间，也指事物发展过程中出现的时机或时运。在"时"所规定的境遇中，有着与之相适应的处事之法。"时"的出现与消失及其对人事的影响，体现着天道、人事的运行法则。人应认识并把握"时"的变化，采取与"时"相适应的行动。

The notion of adjusting one's actions to the "times" comes from *The Book of Changes*. The "times" refer to the opportunities or chances that present themselves as human activities progress. In the circumstances determined by the times, one should choose correspondingly suitable methods of handling affairs. The appearance and disappearance of opportunities and chances, and their impact on human affairs reflect the principles of the way of heaven and human affairs. People should recognize and keep pace with the change of the times and adapt in agreement with the times.

引例 Citations：

◎损益盈虚，与时偕行。(《周易·彖下》)

(减损或增加、充盈或虚亏，都应当依据时机而行动。)

Either to decrease or to increase, to inflate or to deflate: all should go with the times. (*The Book of Changes*)

◎不可必，故待之不可以一方也。唯与时俱化者，为能涉变而常通耳。(郭象《庄子注》卷七)

(不可以偏执，因此不能用单一的原则去对待事物。只有行事与"时"一起变化的人，才能在变化之中始终保持通达。)

One should not be obstinate and thus must not handle different things in the same manner. Only those who go with the times can go through changes while remaining open-minded in their understanding of things. (Guo Xiang: *Annotations on Zhuangzi*)

yuèjiào 乐教

Music Education

　　中国古代借助音乐实施政治教化的方式，与"诗教"相配合。先秦儒家总结周代的音乐教育成果，认为音乐可以移风易俗，感化人心，培养人格，并由此建构了儒家关于音乐及音乐教育的一套完整的理论体系。后"乐教"和"诗教"都是官方教育的重要科目，成为中国古代礼乐文明的重要组成部分。

In ancient China, music, together with poetry, was a way to conduct political education. Reviewing music education in the Zhou Dynasty, the Confucian scholars before the Qin-dynasty unification of China at the time concluded that music could transform social and cultural practices, stir up one's inner emotions, and cultivate a good character. On this basis, they developed a comprehensive Confucian theory of music and music education. Subsequently, both "music education" and "poetry education" became important subjects in the official school system, forming a key part of early Chinese ritual and music culture.

引例 Citations：

◎乐也者，圣人之所乐也。而可以善民心，其感人深，其移风易俗，故先王著其教焉。(《礼记·乐记》)
(音乐是圣人所喜爱的。它可以使人心向善，感人至深，能够移风易俗，因此先王非常注重其教化功能。)

Music is what sages take delight in. It can cultivate goodness, move the people and transform social mores. That is why the past kings valued its role of education. (*The Book of Rites*)

◎夫声乐之入人也深，其化人也速。(《荀子·乐论》)

(音乐能够深深打动人心，让人迅速得到感化。)

Music touches people profoundly; its transformative power is rapid. (*Xunzi*)

záobì-jièguāng 凿壁借光

Borrow Light from a Next Door Neighbor

　　凿穿墙壁，借邻居的烛光照明读书。西汉时期大文学家匡衡年幼家贫，他酷爱读书但家中没有蜡烛供他夜间读书，他就将墙凿开一个洞，借邻居的烛光发奋读书，终成一代学者。作为中国古代著名的励志故事，其意义超越了具体的行为，重在勤学苦读的精神。

By boring a hole in the next door neighbor's wall, he borrows light in order to read. Well-known scholar Kuang Heng in the Western Han Dynasty loved reading but his family was too poor to afford candles for him to read at night, so he chiseled a hole in the next door neighbor's wall to "borrow light" in order to read. He later became a great scholar. As an inspirational story in ancient times, its significance extends beyond the story itself. It tells how important it is to be diligent in gaining knowledge.

引例 Citation：

◎匡衡字稚圭，勤学而无烛。邻舍有烛而不逮，衡乃穿壁引其光，以书映光而读之。(葛洪《西京杂记》卷二)

（匡衡字稚圭，他勤奋好学，但家中没有蜡烛。邻家有蜡烛，但光亮照不到他家，匡衡就在墙壁上凿了洞引来邻家的光亮，借着光亮读书。）

Kuang Heng, also known as Zhigui, was very diligent in his studies but had no candles to allow him to read at night. The next door neighbor had candles but there was no way for him to use the light unless he chiseled a hole in the wall. He did so and was able to read with the ray of light from the next door neighbor. (Ge Hong: *Collection of Miscellaneous Stories in the Western Capital*)

zhèngshēng 郑声

The Music of the State of Zheng

指与"雅乐"相对的民间通俗音乐。原指春秋战国时期郑、卫地区的音乐，又称"郑卫之音"。较之雅乐的庄重、大气、规范，郑声曲调自由、富于形式变化，歌词内容多写男女之情。孔子（前551—前479）认为这些作品放纵个人情感，思想不够纯正，有损礼乐教化，应该加以排斥。后世学者多以"郑声"指代低俗文艺，亦有学者认为它们应该属于民歌等通俗文艺范畴，是艺术创新的源头及对高雅艺术的一种补充。

This refers to popular folk music in history, as opposed to formal ceremonial music. The term, originally "the music of Zheng and Wei," referred to music from the states of Zheng and Wei during the Spring and Autumn and the Warring States periods. Unlike stately, grand and highly structured classical music, the music of Zheng featured free-flowing melodies and a wealth of variations, with lyrics that often spoke of the love between men and women. Confucius (551-479 BC) felt that works of this sort gave free rein to personal emotions and lacked purity in ways of thinking, that they were not conducive to educating people through etiquette and music, and should therefore not be permitted. Many scholars subsequently used "the music of Zheng" to refer to lowbrow arts, but others considered these tunes to be folk songs which were a form of popular culture, a source of artistic creation and a complement to highbrow arts.

引例 Citations：

◎放郑声，远佞人。郑声淫，佞人殆。(《论语·卫灵公》)

（抛弃郑国的音乐，远离花言巧语的小人。郑国的音乐淫靡，花言巧语的小人危险。）

Cast aside the music of Zheng, and keep your distance from smooth-talking petty men. The music of Zheng is seductive, and smooth-talking petty men are dangerous. (*The Analects*)

◎《韶》响难追，郑声易启。岂惟观乐？于焉识礼。(刘勰《文心雕龙·乐府》)

（虞舜时的《韶》乐难以企及，而淫靡俗乐却很容易流行。难道季札当年只是为了想听鲁国的音乐？他是想通过音乐了解礼的兴衰啊。）

Classical music from the era of Yu and Shun is hard to grasp, whereas the crass and seductive music (of Zheng) can easily become popular. Do you think Jizha only wanted to listen to the music of the State of Lu? He wanted to understand, through music, the decline of rites and etiquette. (Liu Xie: *The Literary Mind and the Carving of Dragons*)

zhīcháng-dábiàn 知常达变

Master Both Permanence and Change

既掌握事物的基本规律，又懂得灵活应对具体情况或问题；既坚持原则，又能随机应变。"常"与"变"是中国古代哲学的一对范畴。事物的本质规定性、基本规律、一般原则等具有相对稳定性，故称"常"；具体事物及具体应对方法又有多样性，且随时而化，故称"变"。"常"相对于"变"而言，是存在于"变"之中的常道。"常"是根本，"变"是派生。因此，既要掌握事物的基本规律和一般原则，也要根据客观形势的变化灵活运用这些常道。"知常达变"反映了古人关于普遍性与特殊性、原则性和灵活性辩证统一的认识论和方法论。

This term means one should not only have a good command of the basic rules that govern things, but also know how to deal with exceptional situations or problems in a flexible manner. It suggests that one should not just adhere to principles, but also act according to circumstances. *Chang* (常 permanence) and *bian* (变 change) are two opposing concepts in ancient Chinese philosophy. The nature of things that decides what they are, and their basic rules or general principles that are relatively stable are called *chang* (permanence); but when it comes to specific situations or ways to deal with them, they are different and change in different circumstances, thus they are called *bian* (change). Relative to change, permanence is what endures within change. Permanence is fundamental while change is a deviation. Therefore, one needs not only to have a good command of the basic rules and general principles of things, but also know how to apply these rules and principles in a flexible manner according to objective circumstances. The mastery of both permanence and change reflects ancient Chinese people's perception of both generality and particularity as well as principles and flexibility. It also shows their methodology in the application of both.

引例 Citations：

◎归根曰静，静曰复命。复命曰常，知常曰明。(《老子·十六章》)
(返回事物的本原就叫做"静"，"静"就是回归事物的本来状态。回归事物的本来状态就是"常"，认识了"常"就达到了圣明。)

Returning to the basics leads to tranquility. Tranquility leads to the return of life. The return of life means permanence, and understanding permanence is to be enlightened. (*Laozi*).

◎盖事贵因时而达变，道在取法以自强。(王韬《越南通商御侮说》)
(大凡处理事情贵在根据时机做到灵活变化，最好的办法就是师法 [他国的通商] 以求自强。)

In dealing with matters, it is best to be able to be flexible; the best way is to learn to strive for self-improvement. (Wang Tao: *Vietnam's Resistance against Bullying by France Through Trade with Other European Countries*)

zhì 智

Intelligence

"智"的基本含义是聪明、智慧，本作"知"。"智"的意义主要体现在对是非、利害做出明晰的认知与判断。"智"既是对外在的人与事的认知，也包括对自身的反省。儒家主张，应恰当地发挥"智"的作用，使人们不为复杂的现实因素所迷惑，从而做出符合道德、礼法的选择。而对"智"的过度依赖，则会导致以智巧、欺诈的手段行事，因此道家对于"智"持警惕、批评的态度。

Zhi (智), originally written as zhi (知 a different Chinese character representing knowing), means intelligence. It suggests clear cognition and good judgment of right and wrong, advantage and disadvantage. Intelligence shows both one's awareness of other people and events as well as one's ability to conduct introspection. Confucianism believes that people should have intelligence so as not to be confused by complexities of life and be able to act in conformity with ethical and ritual standards. However, excessive use of intelligence may lead to deception and fraud. Therefore, Daoists tend to view intelligence with suspicion and disapproval.

引例 Citations：

◎恻隐之心，仁之端也；羞恶之心，义之端也；辞让之心，礼之端也；是非之心，智之端也。(《孟子·公孙丑上》)

(恻隐之心是仁的端始，羞耻厌恶之心是义的端始，辞让之心是礼的端始，辨明是非之心是智的端始。)

Compassion gives rise to benevolence; detestation leads to righteousness; deference fosters propriety, and good judgment of right and wrong creates intelligence. (Mencius)

◎故以智治国，国之贼；不以智治国，国之福。(《老子·六十五章》)

(因此用巧智来治理国家，是国家的祸患；不用巧智来治理国家，是国家的福祉。)

He who governs with overuse of intelligence brings peril to the country; he who governs without overuse of intelligence brings prosperity to it. (Laozi)

术语表 List of Concepts

英文	中文
A Journey of a Thousand *Li* Begins with the First Step.	千里之行，始于足下
A Man of Virtue Maintains His Ideals Even in Frustrations.	君子固穷
A Single Remark Makes a Country Prosper.	一言兴邦
Affection for One's Kin	亲亲
All Things Have a Beginning, but Few Can Reach the End.	靡不有初，鲜克有终
Artistic Appeal	气韵
Assess Governance by Listening to Music	审音知政
Be as Loyal as One Can Be and Serve One's Own Country	尽忠报国
Be Completely Convinced and Follow Willingly	心悦诚服
Be Content with a Simple but Virtuous Life	安贫乐道
Be Discreet as if Standing on Cliff Edge or Treading on Thin Ice	临渊履薄
Borrow Light from a Next Door Neighbor	凿壁借光
Bright but Not Dazzling	光而不耀
Build Up Fully and Release Sparingly	厚积薄发
Caring for Others Is the Top Priority.	爱人为大
Change Along with Times	时序
Compare Appearances to Grasp the Essence	拟容取心
Constant and Temporary	经 / 权

英文	中文
Convey the Spirit and Capture the Person	传神写照
Courage	勇
Court Calculation	庙算
Cultivate Virtue and Strengthen the Army	修德振兵
Daxue (Great Learning)	大学
Deliver Extensive Benefits to the People and Relieve the Suffering of the Poor	博施济众
Establish Credibility Through Careful Choice of Words	修辞立诚
Establish One's Credibility by Rewarding People for Moving a Log	徙木立信
Exaggeration and Embellishment	夸饰
Express the Ideas in Earlier Literary Works in a New Way	夺胎换骨
Extend Benevolence and Love	推恩
Extreme – Change – Continuity	穷则变，变则通，通则久
Fleshy Body and Soft Bone Structure	丰肉微骨
Give One's Life to Uphold Righteousness	舍生取义
Go with the Times	与时偕行
Good Faith	信
Harmonious Combination of Eight Sounds	八音克谐
Harmony Comes from Appropriateness.	和出于适

英文	中文
Have a Complete Image of the Bamboo Before Drawing It / Have a Fully Formed Picture in the Mind's Eye	成竹于胸
History	史
Illustrious Virtue	明德
Inconspicuous Virtue	玄德
Influence Others Without Preaching	不言之教
Inspirational Creation Based on Association in Thinking	迁想妙得
Intelligence	智
Introspection	反求诸己
It Takes Ten Years to Grow Trees and a Hundred Years to Nurture Talents.	十年树木，百年树人
Keep Good Faith and Pursue Harmony	讲信修睦
Keep Wealth with the People	藏富于民
Land of Peach Blossoms / Land of Idyllic Beauty	世外桃源
Laws Change Along with Evolving Times; Rites Shift Along with Changing Customs.	法与时变，礼与俗化
Lunar Year / Year	年
Maintain Originality and Embrace Simplicity	见素抱朴
Make Appraisals	品题
Master Both Permanence and Change	知常达变
Moral Character Can Be Built by Accumulating Goodness.	积善成德
Music Education	乐教
Natural Attribute	性分

英文	中文
Natural, Leisurely, Simple yet Profound	萧散简远
Northern Opera	北曲
Observe a Fundamental Principle Throughout One's Pursuit	一以贯之
Ornate Parallel Style	丽辞
Painstaking Versification	苦吟
Paradox of the Spear and the Shield / Contradiction	矛盾
People of Similar Natures and Emotions Will Have Similar Understanding.	心同理同
Physical Form Gives Birth to Spirit.	形具神生
Pool Wisdom of the People	集思广益
Promises Must Be Kept; Actions Must Be Resolute.	言必信，行必果
Proper Ranking Leads to Collaboration.	明分使群
Put Oneself in Another's Place	推己及人
Qi or *Zheng* (Surprise or Normal)	奇正
Recover from a Social Upheaval and Restore Production / Develop Economy and Increase Population	休养生息
Reflect on Oneself Several Times a Day	三省吾身
Rejoice in Complying with Heaven and Know Its Mandate	乐天知命
Relying on Force and Flaunting One's Superiority Leads to Destruction.	兵强则灭
See the Way with One's Own Eyes	目击道存

英文	中文
Seek Common Ground While Setting Aside Differences	求同存异
Sensed Externalities	感物
Separate Hardness from Whiteness	离坚白
Six Criteria	六观
Six Rules of Painting	绘画六法
Sounds of Nature	天籁
Southern Opera	南戏
Spring Festival	春节
The Best Strategy in Warfare is to Foil the Enemy's Strategy.	上兵伐谋
The Chinese Zodiac / Animal of the Year	生肖
The Foolish Old Man Who Moved the Mountains	愚公移山
The Music of the State of Zheng	郑声
The Qingming Festival	清明
The Six Arts	六艺
The Twenty-four Solar Terms	节气
The White Silk First, the Painting Afterwards / Beauty from Natural Simplicity	绘事后素
Three Friends of Winter / Steadfast, Loyal Friends	岁寒三友
Tie One's Hair on the House Beam and Jab One's Side with an Awl to Keep Oneself from Falling Asleep while Studying	悬梁刺股
Time / Timing	时

英文	中文
Transcend the Outer Form to Capture the Essence	离形得似
Transform Intrinsic Evil Nature to Develop Acquired Nature of Goodness	化性起伪
Truth in Imagination	幻中有真
Tyranny Is Fiercer than a Tiger.	苛政猛于虎
Unify Similarity and Difference	合同异
Use Stones from Another Mountain to Polish One's Jade	他山之石，可以攻玉
When Drinking Water, One Must Not Forget Its Source.	饮水思源

中国历史年代简表 A Brief Chronology of Chinese History

夏 Xia Dynasty		2070-1600 BC
商 Shang Dynasty		1600-1046 BC
周 Zhou Dynasty		1046-256 BC
周 Zhou Dynasty	西周 Western Zhou Dynasty	1046-771 BC
	东周 Eastern Zhou Dynasty	770-256 BC
秦 Qin Dynasty		221-206 BC
汉 Han Dynasty		206 BC-AD 220
汉 Han Dynasty	西汉 Western Han Dynasty	206 BC-AD 25
	东汉 Eastern Han Dynasty	25-220
三国 Three Kingdoms		220-280
三国 Three Kingdoms	魏 Kingdom of Wei	220-265
	蜀 Kingdom of Shu	221-263
	吴 Kingdom of Wu	222-280
晋 Jin Dynasty		265-420
晋 Jin Dynasty	西晋 Western Jin Dynasty	265-317
	东晋 Eastern Jin Dynasty	317-420
南北朝 Southern and Northern Dynasties		420-589
南北朝 Southern and Northern Dynasties	南朝 Southern Dynasties	420-589
	南朝 Southern Dynasties — 宋 Song Dynasty	420-479
	齐 Qi Dynasty	479-502
	梁 Liang Dynasty	502-557
	陈 Chen Dynasty	557-589

南北朝 Southern and Northern Dynasties	北朝 Northern Dynasties	北朝 Northern Dynasties	386-581
		北魏 Northern Wei Dynasty	386-534
		东魏 Eastern Wei Dynasty	534-550
		北齐 Northern Qi Dynasty	550-577
		西魏 Western Wei Dynasty	535-556
		北周 Northern Zhou Dynasty	557-581
隋 Sui Dynasty			581-618
唐 Tang Dynasty			618-907
五代 Five Dynasties			907-960
五代 Five Dynasties	后梁 Later Liang Dynasty		907-923
	后唐 Later Tang Dynasty		923-936
	后晋 Later Jin Dynasty		936-947
	后汉 Later Han Dynasty		947-950
	后周 Later Zhou Dynasty		951-960
宋 Song Dynasty			960-1279
宋 Song Dynasty	北宋 Northern Song Dynasty		960-1127
	南宋 Southern Song Dynasty		1127-1279
辽 Liao Dynasty			907-1125
西夏 Western Xia Dynasty			1038-1227
金 Jin Dynasty			1115-1234
元 Yuan Dynasty			1206-1368
明 Ming Dynasty			1368-1644
清 Qing Dynasty			1616-1911
中华民国 Republic of China			1912-1949
中华人民共和国 People's Republic of China			Founded on October 1, 1949